THE BOOK
FOR EVERY REFERENCE SHELF

How to Achieve Competence in English is brief
and practical. It contains entries as specific as
bibliography, colons, envelopes, footnotes, prefixes, roots of ~~~~~~~~~~~~~~~~~~. It also
contains ~~~~~~~~~~~~~~~~~~~~~ as:

- ~~~~~~~~
- ~~~~~~~~
- ~~~~~~~~
- ~~~~~~~~
- proofreading
- speech-making
- transitions
- vocabulary building

This handbook will prove useful to people with
various writing tasks; to entire classes in English;
to academic departments in need of a reasonable
set of standards; and to anyone, out of school or
in, who needs a quick reference book when questions come up about the use of English.

Bette Garrelts.

ABOUT THE AUTHOR

ERIC W. JOHNSON is a teacher at the Germantown Friends School in Philadelphia and is the author of several English and education textbooks. Particularly well known for his work in sex education, he has published three very successful books in this field for junior and senior high school students. Those books include *Love and Sex in Plain Language*, *VD*, and *Sex: Telling It Straight*. Two of his new books, *Life Into Language* and *Worlds Into Words*, designed to stimulate students to think, discuss and write, will be cross-referenced with his third new book, *How to Achieve Competence in English*.

How to Achieve Competence in English

A Quick-Reference Handbook

Eric W. Johnson

Illustrated by Howard S. L. Coale

BANTAM BOOKS · TORONTO · NEW YORK · LONDON

RLI: VLM 8 (VLR 7–8)
IL 8–adult

HOW TO ACHIEVE COMPETENCE IN ENGLISH:
A QUICK REFERENCE HANDBOOK
A Bantam Book / December 1976

Bantam Books are published by Bantam Books, Inc. Its trademark, consisting of the words "Bantam Books" and the portrayal of a bantam, is registered in the United States Patent Office and in other countries. Marca Registrada. Bantam Books, Inc., 666 Fifth Avenue, New York, New York 10019.

PRINTED IN THE UNITED STATES OF AMERICA

0 9 8 7 6 5 4 3

PREFACE

This book is brief and practical. It is not a course of study, although it can be used to back up a course of study. It provides a quick, simple, practical way to look up whatever you need to know, either because you have never learned it or because you have forgotten it. It aims to be useful for people from age ten to senility.

The book contains concise explanations, many examples, no exercises. Everything is arranged alphabetically for quick use; an index of large letters printed on the edge of each page makes entries in the book even easier to find. The book contains entries as specific as "bibliography," "colons," "dashes," "footnotes," "letters," "prefixes," "roots of words," "spelling demons," "syllabication," and "underlining"; you may want to look up any of these for particular information. The book also contains some longer, more general articles under headings you might not expect. Some of these are:

> books
> clichés
> conventions of English
> debating
> essays
> figurative language
> frame tests
> grammar
> language
> libraries
> marks
> memorization
> mnemonic devices
> note-taking
> organization
> parallel construction
> persuasion
> plagiarism
> plays
> poetry

proofreading
purpose
reading
reports
reviewing for tests and exams
sentences
short stories
speech making
spelling
study skills
symbols to guide revision of papers
taking tests and exams
tenses
titles
transitions
vocabulary building
writing for whom?

I suggest that you look up a few of these entries to get an idea of the sort of material that is at your disposal.

A book that is as strictly alphabetized as this one is needs many cross references, and there are scores of them shown thus:

Predicates   see SENTENCES
Editing   see REVISION OF PAPERS; PROOFREADING
Metaphors   see FIGURATIVE LANGUAGE

It is also *important to remember* that any word in the text set in this type—for example, PREPOSITIONS—is the subject of a separate alphabetized entry, where more information can be found.

At the end of each letter section are one or more lined pages on which you can write information, definitions, reminders, spelling, or vocabulary words that will be useful to you.

I have tried throughout to avoid theoretical discussions and to emphasize common usage. However, I have taught English in grades five through twelve for over twenty-five years and am thus well aware that English teachers and linguists disagree among themselves as to just what common usage is. Where an opinion is needed, I give one simply because a sensible opinion is usually better than none. If you disagree with the opinion, no harm. Do it your way if you have reason to. As Mark Twain said, "Loyalty to petrified opinion never yet broke a chain or freed a human soul."

I think the book will be useful to people who are faced with various writing tasks, whether in English class or elsewhere; to entire classes in English and in other subjects, in school or college; to academic departments that need a reasonable set of suggestions and standards to use throughout an academic institution; and to anyone, in school or out of it, who needs a quick-reference handbook when questions come up about writing, and to some extent about speaking, English.

ERIC W. JOHNSON

ACKNOWLEDGMENTS

I have benefited from general and detailed criticism of the manuscript of this book by six people deeply involved in the teaching of English and the creation of materials to be used by students and teachers in English classrooms. To these people go my thanks for saving me from sins of commission and omission.

Morton Botel, Levittown, Pa.; Professor of Education, University of Pennsylvania; formerly Reading and English Supervisor, Bucks County, Pa., Schools; Past President, International Reading Association.

Ellen Medkeff, Lower Merion, Pa.; Chairman, English Department, Lower Merion High School.

Miriam Weiss Meyer, North Tarrytown, N.Y.; Senior Editor, Educational Division, *Reader's Digest;* formerly language arts textbook editor, Harcourt Brace Jovanovich.

Jerry E. Reed, Denver; Supervisor of English, K-12, Denver Public Schools; test developer, Educational Testing Service, Princeton, N.J.; co-author, *Our English Language.*

Ruth E. Reeves, Belair, Texas; author: *The Teaching of Reading in Our Schools; Approaches to Writing; Composition in Action;* editor: *Ideas for Teaching English in Junior High* (NCTE); retired Director of English in Secondary Schools, Houston, Texas.

Richard Tyre, Gladwyne, Pa.; Curriculum Coordinator, Upper Darby (Pa.) Senior High School; formerly: Assistant Professor of Humanities and Literature, Reed College, Portland, Oregon; Supervisor of Teachers, M.A.T. Program, Yale University; Chairman, English Department, Moorestown Friends School.

Eric W. Johnson

abbreviations

An abbreviation of a word is a shortening of it, as *prep.* for *preposition* or *Dr.* for *Doctor*. Abbreviations are followed by a period.

A common writing error is to overabbreviate. You will not go too far wrong if you avoid abbreviations except where they are conventional, as *Dr.*, *Mr.*, *Mrs.*, names of states in addresses, A.M., P.M., and the like. See also PERIOD, 2.

addresses

In writing out addresses, every item after the first is enclosed by commas.

> *Example:*
> My uncle lives at 3752 Chunk Street, Peach Bottom, Pennsylvania 17563, where he has a small business.
>
> NOTE: There is no comma between the state and the zip-code number; a comma is placed at the end of the address (unless it comes at the end of a sentence, in which case the period takes its place). For addresses in letters and on envelopes, see LETTERS.

adjective clauses   see CLAUSES, A.

adjectives

An adjective is a word used to modify NOUNS or PRONOUNS (see also MODIFIERS). It is one of the PARTS OF SPEECH. It often answers the questions *what kind*?

1

A

(descriptive adjective), *which one*? or *how many*? or *how much*?

Examples:

1. The *green* soup was *disgusting*. [what kind?]

2. She looked at *that* boy with interest. [which one?]

3. *Five* geniuses made *several* errors. [how many? how much?]

4. The house looks *spooky*. [what kind?]

Adjectives telling *what kind* can be compared (see COMPARISON OF ADJECTIVES AND ADVERBS).

Here are some FRAME TESTS for adjectives.

1. The _____ thing came near.
       (adjective)

2. The thing was very _____.
                       (adjective)

3. _____ apples are needed to make a pie.
   (adjective)

See also PHRASES, A.

adverbials   see ADVERBS.

adverbs

An adverb is a word used to modify a VERB, ADJECTIVE, or another adverb (see also MODIFIERS). It is one of the PARTS OF SPEECH. Most adverbs modify verbs. An adverb often answers the question *how*?, *where*?, *when*?, or *to what extent*?

Examples:

1. He ate *enthusiastically*. [how?]

2. She *calmly* pushed him into the pool. [how?]

3. He sank *there*. [where?]

2

4. The paper arrived *late*. [when?]

5. *Yesterday* my mother had a fit. [when?]

6. Please *never* eat rabbit in my house. [to what extent?]

7. The speaker droned on *forever*. [to what extent?]

NOTES:

1. Many adverbs are simply a combination of an ADJECTIVE and the ending -*ly*: *bright* [adj.], *brightly* [adv.]; *calm, calmly*. Such adverbs generally answer the question *how?* and can be compared (see COMPARISON OF ADJECTIVES AND ADVERBS).

2. A limited number of adverbs modify adjectives and other adverbs. This special class of adverbs works in sentences like the word *very*. In recent grammars these adverbs are called QUALIFIERS or *intensifiers*. They cannot be compared. The most common is *very*. Other examples are *rather, somewhat, too*.

3. Adverbs can be moved about in sentences. For example:

   Usually, the President of the United States is not a crook.

   The President of the United States *usually* is not a crook.

   The President of the United States is *usually* not a crook.

   The President of the United States is not a crook *usually*.

4. An *adverbial* is a group of words used like an adverb—that is, to modify a verb (see CLAUSES, B; PHRASES, A).

Here are two FRAME TESTS for adverbs except QUALIFIERS:

1. He said it _____.
   (adverb)

2. He _____ said it.
   (adverb)

A

agreement of subjects and verbs

SUBJECTS and VERBS must agree in number in all SENTENCES: that is, if the subject is singular, the singular form of the verb must be used; if plural, plural. (*Singular* means one only; *plural* means more than one.)

> *Examples:*
>
> 1. The *pupils* all   *sleep*   duri g class.
>   (plural subject)   (plural verb)
>
> 2. *One*   of the boys   *beats*
>   (singular subject)   (singular verb)
>
>   up weaklings.
>
> 3. *He*   *doesn't*   like it.
>   (singular subject)   (singular verb)
>
> NOTE: Usually nouns add an *s* or *es* to form their plurals, while an *s* ending on a verb usually shows that it is singular.

announcements   see SPEECH-MAKING.

apostrophes   see also FIGURATIVE LANGUAGE, C.

The apostrophe is used for two purposes.

A. The apostrophe indicates possession.

1. When the possessive noun is singular, add *'s*. (The *cat's* collar is too tight); (the *girl's* dress is short.)
2. When the possessive noun is plural and ends in *s*, add apostrophe only. (*Girls'* sports deserve facilities equal to *boys'*.)
3. When the possessive noun is plural and does not end in *s*, add *'s*. (The *men's, women's,* and *children's* shouts brought the police.)
4. If the possessive noun is singular and ends in *s*, add either *'s* or *'* only. (*Charles's* tonsils were larger than *Mrs. Jones's.*) Or: (*Charles'* Honda was faster than *Mr. Jones'* tricycle.)
   NOTE: After you have chosen a form, use it consistently.

B. The apostrophe is used to show that a word has

4

been contracted or shortened. Use an apostrophe in a contraction at the place where letters have been omitted.

1. *Music's* the medicine of a troubled mind. [Music is]
2. Please *don't* eat the daisies. [do not]

Other common contractions are cannot = *can't*; it is = *it's*; who is = *who's*; she is = *she's*; of the clock = *o'clock*.

appositives   see also PHRASES, C.

An appositive is a word or phrase within a SEN-TENCE that follows a NOUN and gives information about it.

Examples:

1. This handbook, *a dull but useful volume*, should not be burned at the end of the year.
2. Fido's barking awoke Smirk, *the neighborhood grouch*.

Appositives are set off from the rest of the sentence by commas, except when they are short and when there is no pause before them.

Example:

The painter *Michelangelo* ate clams.

> NOTE: A group of words that begins with *who* or *which* is not an appositive but a *clause*. It contains a subject and a verb; an appositive does not.
> *Example:*
> Sara Ogle,   *who arrived late,*   was spurned.
>   (a clause, not an appositive)

articles

The words *a, an,* and *the* are PARTS OF SPEECH called articles. They are the most frequently used ADJECTIVES. They are also called DETERMINERS.

audience for writing   See WRITING FOR WHOM?

auxiliary verbs   see VERBS, C.

A

be   see VERBS, B.

beginning, middle, and end   see ESSAYS, C.

bibliography

In writing REPORTS you will probably use books and magazines as source material. At the end of the paper you should list your sources in a *bibliography*, arranged alphabetically by each author's last name. Each entry in a bibliography should include information as to the author, title, place of publication, publisher and date of publication of your source. For magazines and newspapers, specify the title of the article you read, and if there is one, list the volume number of the publication from which this article is drawn after you write the name of the publication. While there are a number of acceptable ways of listing information in a bibliography, the following is perhaps the most common:

> *book*   Mailer, Norman, *The Fight*. Boston: Little, Brown and Company, 1975.
>
> *magazine*   Dubrow, Marsha. "Female Assertiveness: How a Pussycat Can Learn to Be a Panther." *New York Magazine*, July 28, 1975.

> NOTE: Titles of books and names of magazines are underlined (italicized); titles of articles or chapters in magazines or books are enclosed in quotation marks.

B

books

A student recently said, "Books are the best teaching machines there are." They are compact, convenient, durable, comparatively inexpensive, and they don't get out of order. The British historian Thomas Carlyle called them "by far the most momentous, wonderful, and worthy" objects that people can make, and the American writer Jesse Lee Bennett said, "Books are the compasses and telescopes and sextants and charts . . . to help us navigate the dangerous seas of human life."

Here are a few facts that will enable you to navigate the contents of books.

A. *The table of contents*

At the front of most nonfiction and some works of fiction there is a table of contents listing the titles of sections and chapters of the book. Reading it will give you an overview of the book, help you decide if it is one you want or need to read, and show how the various parts of the book fit into the whole.

B. *The index*

Nonfiction books often end with an index, which is simply an alphabetical list of topics, subjects, and names covered in the text. If you need to know whether a specific piece of information can be found in a book, or where to find it, use the index.

C. *Preface or introduction*

Many books open with a preface, introduction, or foreword in which the author explains the nature of the book, his purpose in writing it, and the readers for whom he thinks it will be of value. Although his judgment of the value of the book may not be entirely objective, what he says may help you benefit from the book—or it may even make you decide not to read it.

D. *Copyright notice*

At the very front of the book is the *title page*, which lists the title, author, and publisher of the book. On the back of this page is given the copyright date—when the book was finished and sent to the Library of Congress (for books published in the USA) for copyrighting. It will probably look like this: © 1975. Sometimes there are several dates, the latest one being that of the most recent revision, major or minor. It is often important to know when a book was written so that you can tell whether the information in it is up to date.

See also LIBRARIES; READING; STUDY SKILLS.

brackets ([ ])

Brackets are used in two situations.

A. Brackets indicate that your own words are inserted or substituted within a quotation.

Example:

Samuel Johnson wrote in 1775: "There is now less flogging in our great schools than formerly,—but then less is learned there, so that what the boys get [win] at one end they lose at the other."

B. Brackets indicate a parenthetical expression within a set of PARENTHESES.

Example:

The King James Version of the Bible (provided in most hotel rooms by Gideons International [see the article on page 356]) is written in the English of the seventeenth century.

business letters   see LETTERS, C.

_____

_____

_____

_____

B

capitalization

In general, capitalize (a) the first word of any sentence; (b) the pronoun *I*; and (c) any proper noun—that is, any word that is a name: "Mississippi," "Bob." It is also important to know when *not* to capitalize.

A. *When to capitalize*

    1. Capitalize the names of months, days of the week, and holidays (but *not* the names of the four seasons).

Examples:

December	spring
April	summer
Tuesday	autumn
Saturday	fall
Easter	winter
Washington's Birthday	

    2. Capitalize the names of particular organizations, schools, colleges, universities, buildings, and companies.

Examples:

the International Red Cross
Central High School
City University of New York
the Philadelphia Mint
Potomac Electric Company

    3. Capitalize the names of particular historic events, documents, and periods.

Examples:

the American Revolution

World War II
the Declaration of Independence
the Communist Manifesto
the Renaissance
the Middle Ages
4. Capitalize the names of particular brands or products.

Examples:
Skipslow Peanut Butter
Snap 'n' Crackle Chewies
5. Capitalize the names of religions, races, nationalities, and languages.

Examples:
the Presbyterian Church
the Roman Catholic Church
Caucasian
Negroid
Negro [whether or not you capitalize *black* when referring to Negro is a matter of choice]
French, English, Nigerian
Swahili, Urdu, Esperanto
6. Capitalize words that show a person's family relationship, rank, title, office, or profession when they are used with a person's name. Capitalize them if they are used as a name or form of address. Usually no DETERMINER precedes the word when it is used as a name.

Examples:
Uncle Ezra, Cousin Molly
Colonel Bush, Sergeant York
Congressman Fernaldo, Senator Vastform, Governor Trask
Superintendent Atkins
"Come here, Mother."
7. Capitalize the titles of important office-holders.

Examples:

the President of the United States

the Secretary of State

8. Capitalize geographical names such as those of states, nations, parks, lakes, oceans, cities or streets.

Examples:

Massachusetts, Nevada

Ghana, the Soviet Union

Central Park, Fairmount Park

Lake Superior, Lake Baikal

the Pacific Ocean, the Mediterranean Sea

Chicago, Little Rock

Sesame Street, Swedesford Road

9. Capitalize the first, last and all important words in title. A *verb* in a title is always important, even if it is short—*Is, Am, See,* and the like.

Examples:

Zen and the Art of Motorcycle Maintenance

"Arnold Knocks the Dragon Down"

"The Night the Ghost Got In"

Mad

The New York Review of Books

the *Mona Lisa*

10. Capitalize words referring to God.

Example:

Praise God and give thanks to Him for His many blessings.

11. In LETTERS, capitalize the salutation and the first word of the complimentary close.

Examples:

Dear Sir

Dear Carlos

Very truly yours

Sincerely yours

12. Capitalize the first word in each line of conventional POETRY.

Example:

The downpour prickles on the pond, so sharp
It hits the heads of shallow-floating carp.

—SHIKI

NOTE: Many modern poets do not follow this rule, using capitals only according to standard prose rules, or sometimes none at all.

13. Capitalize school subjects *only* when they are languages or the names of particular courses.

Examples:

Spanish

Ancient African Civilizations

Biology 2

history

biology

14. Capitalize the first word spoken in DIALOGUE.

Example:

John said, "Please look away."

B. *When not to capitalize*

In general, never capitalize unless you have a reason to. The reason may be one of the rules above or because you wish to create a special effect.

1. Do *not* capitalize the names of animals, birds, flowers, trees, diseases, games, foods, and seasons unless they contain a PROPER NOUN [Tay-Sachs disease] or PROPER ADJECTIVE [English sparrow].

2. Do *not* capitalize such words as *senior class* or *upper school* unless they form a special name.

Example:

Junior High School Spring Dance

3. Do *not* capitalize NOUNS that follow a brand name unless they are a part of the name.

Examples:

Ford car, Kleenex tissue, Spearmint gum; but Toaster Tarts, the Volkswagen Rabbit

4. Do *not* capitalize points of the compass [east, south, north, west] except when referring to a region or a political entity.

Examples:

The East defeated the West in the play-off.

The North won the Civil War.

the Eastern bloc nations

5. Do *not* capitalize *a, an,* or *the* before a title or name unless they are a part of the title or name.

Examples:

the St. Louis *Post-Dispatch*; the *National Enquirer*; the Right Honorable Senator from Maine; *The Time Machine, Intruder in the Dust.*

6. Writers often have difficulty deciding whether or not to capitalize such words as *mother, father, uncle, aunt.* In general, do *not* capitalize them if they are not used as a name.

Example:

My *m*other married my *f*ather in the presence of two *a*unts and my old *g*randmother.

card catalog   see LIBRARIES, B.

cases

In English, NOUNS and PRONOUNS have three cases (or forms): the SUBJECT case (often called the *subjective* or the *nominative* case), the OBJECT case (or *objective* case) and the *possessive* case. The case or form of a noun or pronoun is determined by how the word is used in a sentence. See also DIRECT OBJECT; INDIRECT OBJECT; SENTENCES.

Examples:

subject case	1. *I* groaned with pain.
	2. Afterward *we* ate a gopher.
object case	1. The hero loved *her*.
	2. She didn't love *him*.

possessive case   *Joe's* toe is twisted. So is *mine*.
Hers came completely off.

C

NOTE: An understanding of case is especially useful in determining the form of *pronouns*. See PRONOUNS, chart.

clauses

A clause is a group of related words that contains a SUBJECT and a VERB.

Clauses can be classified in several ways; the following distinctions are of the most use to the writer of general material.

A. *independent* or *main clause*. This is the same as a SENTENCE.

> *Example:*
> *Molly was blowing* bubble gum.
> (subject) (verb)

B. *dependent* or *subordinate clause*. This is a clause that cannot "stand alone"; it needs the rest of the sentence to complete it.

> *Examples:*
> 1. While Molly was blowing bubble gum, there
>   (subj.) (verb)
>   —— subordinate clause ——
>
>   was a loud pop.
> 2. The girl who gave me a dirty look was
>   (subj.) (verb)
>   subordinate clause ——
>
>   distressingly intelligent.

Two common types of the subordinate clause are the *adjective clause* and the *adverb clause*.

A. An *adjective clause* modifies a noun in a sentence.

> *Examples:*
>
> 1. Mrs. Jones, *who likes our dog,* rescued him from the dog catcher.
>
> 2. That historical novel, *which is long and complicated,* caught my interest.
>
> 3. Cars *that guzzle gas* impoverish drivers.

16

NOTES:
1. Generally the word *who* introduces adjective clauses that refer to people, the word *which* to things, and the word *that* to things or people or both.
2. For punctuation of adjective clauses within a sentence, see RESTRICTIVE CLAUSES.

B. An *adverb clause* modifies a verb in a sentence.
   Examples:

1. I *like* you *because you never scold me.*
   (verb)

2. *Although Bob likes me,* he *shouts* at my father.

Adverb clauses are introduced by a word called a *subordinator* (or *subordinating* CONJUNCTION). Some common subordinates are: *after, although, because, if, since, so that, unless, until, when, whenever,* and *while.* If you put a subordinator in front of a sentence, the result is a subordinate clause.

   Example:
1. *Sentence*   My house is my castle.
2. *Subordinate Clause*   *unless* my house is my castle . . .

The idea of the subordinate clause sounds as if it needs to be completed: *"Unless my house is my castle, I'm going to move into your house."*

NOTES:
1. When a subordinate clause begins a sentence, it is usually set off from the rest of the sentence by a comma (as in the example just above).
2. Much of our DIALOGUE—conversation—is made up of subordinate clauses. We do not always speak in complete sentences. However, unless you are writing realistic DIALOGUE or want to achieve a special effect, always use complete sentences.

clichés

A cliché is a trite, hackneyed expression that has been used so much that it has become weak and unconvincing.

Examples:
big as a house
a fluffy cloud
the silvery moon
keep the wolf from the door
grin and bear it
quick as lightning
slow as molasses in January

A cliché (a French word meaning, among other things, a rubber stamp) may have been effective the first few times it was used, but it has become stale. When writing, try for fresh ways of saying things. A high-school student illustrated the point—perhaps too graphically—in the following two verses.

B.C. *(Before Cliché)*

Morning
I watched a fluffy cloud drift by
Across the boundless blue of sky
And saw the sun's rays, molten gold,
Upon the dewy earth unfold!

Evening
I felt my fettered soul uplift
Before the rosy sunset drift
And in the hazy blue afar,
I saw the gleaming evening star.

A.D. *(After Discovering)*

Morning
I saw the sun with battered face
Trying to warm the human race;
I watched a sodden cloud limp by
Like some discouraged custard pie.

Evening
The sleepy sun in flannels red
Went yawning to its western bed;
I saw one shivering small star
No brighter than our dishpans are.

18

colons (:)

A colon calls the reader's attention to what comes next; it indicates that something is to follow.

Examples:
1. The results were very bad: nothing to eat for three days, four people down with pneumonia, and over $500 worth of lost equipment.
2. In life there are four things people can do with their hands: wring them in despair, fold them in apathy, put them in their pockets for safekeeping, or lay them on a job that needs doing.

The colon is also used:
1. to introduce a list [such as the following: flashlight, raincoat, rabbit's foot . . .]
2. after the salutation in a formal letter [Dear Sir: Gentlemen: Dear Ms. Pressler:]
3. in writing the time [6:25 P.M.]
4. in separating chapter and verse in Bible citations [Luke 3:7]

commas (,)

The comma is used to separate items from each other, especially in sentences.

A. Use a comma to separate two SENTENCES joined by a coordinating CONJUNCTION [and, but, or, for].

Example:
Francis thinks the food in the cafeteria is pure poison, *and* Jeffrey wants to know why they serve such small helpings.

> NOTE: If the two sentences are very short, no comma is required.
> *Example:*
> John smoked and Mary fumed.

B. The comma is never used when there is only one sentence with a single SUBJECT and a compound VERB—that is, where the *and* or *but* do not separate two complete sentences.

Example:
George *saw* himself in a mirror and *was* quite
(subject) (verb) (verb)

19

C

upset.

C. The comma is used to set off APPOSITIVE PHRASES.

Example:

My guest, *an old Chinese gentleman,* asked why football wasn't played by coolies.

D. The comma is generally used to set off introductory PHRASES or CLAUSES from the rest of the sentence.

Examples:

1. *Between the tree and bush,* a small crocus was growing. [phrase]
2. *After he had washed himself carefully,* Albert fell in the muck. [clause]
3. *Because the dog was awake,* he bit the thief. [clause]

E. Words in direct address are set off by commas.

Examples:

1. *John,* what do you think?
2. Oh, *God,* make the bad people good and the good people nice.
3. We saw you, *Frank,* at the game.

F. Commas are used to set off such words as *yes, no, well, however,* when they are used alone at the beginning of a sentence.

Examples:

1. *Yes,* I think so.
2. *However,* she did it poorly.
3. *Well,* let me think.

G. Set off interrupting expressions by commas.

Examples:

1. Little Boy Blue, *on the other hand,* did not lose his head.
2. It's better, *I suppose,* to lose your sheep.
3. These are, *as Tom Paine wrote in 1776,* the times that try men's souls.

H. Set off restrictive clauses by commas, but not nonrestrictive clauses. See RESTRICTIVE AND NON-RESTRICTIVE CLAUSE for examples.

I. Use commas to separate items in a SERIES.
Example:
Hooray for the red, white, and blue.

J. In DATES and ADDRESSES, each item after the first one is set off by commas. See also LETTERS.

comparison of adjectives and adverbs

ADJECTIVES and most ADVERBS have three degrees of comparison: the positive, the comparative, and the superlative. The comparative compares two items, the superlative three or more.

Examples:

	positive degree	comparative degree	superlative degree
adjectives	big	bigger	biggest
	ugly	uglier	ugliest
	enormous	more enormous	most enormous
	terrible	more terrible	most terrible
adverbs	soon	sooner	soonest
	quietly	more quietly	most quietly
	interestingly	more interestingly	most interestingly

NOTES:

1. *Less* and *least* can be used instead of *more* and *most.*
   Example:
   The group was *less raucous* than yesterday and the *least attractive* of all the groups in town.

2. One- and two-syllable words are usually compared by adding *-er* or *-est* [happier, happiest].

3. Words of three or more syllables use *more* or *most* [most ridiculous—*not* ridiculous-est].

4. When comparing two items, use the comparative degree.

21

C

Example:
The male twin was *healthier* than the female
When comparing three or more items, use the superlative degree.
Example:
The last-born triplet was the *puniest*.

complements

A *complement* is the word or expression that completes a statement and gives it meaning. Complements are often nouns and are frequently the object of the verb.

Examples:
1. He saw the *ocean*.
2. The ocean was *blue*.
3. It was the *Atlantic*.

See also VERBS, B.

complex sentences
see SIMPLE, COMPOUND, AND COMPLEX SENTENCES, C.

compositions
see ESSAYS and REPORTS.

compound sentences
see SIMPLE, COMPOUND, AND COMPLEX SENTENCES, B.

conjunctions

A conjunction joins words or groups of words. The most common conjunctions are *and, but* and *or*; they are called *coordinating conjunctions*. They join grammatically equal elements—words with words, PHRASES with phrases, SENTENCES with sentences.

Examples:
1. good *or* bad [word with word]
2. in the store *but* out of sight [phrase with phrase]
3. We ate hot tamales, *and* they had cottage cheese. [sentence with sentence; see COMMAS, [A]

22

Another type of conjunction is the *subordinating conjunction*. See CLAUSES, B; COMMA, D.

context

Context refers to the words surrounding a word in a sentence or situation in which the word is used. The context of a word will often help to give you its meaning or tell you which of its several meanings the writer intends. For example, if you did not know the meaning of *enervated*, you could nevertheless understand it in the context of the sentence, "After three days without food, he was so enervated that he could not climb the last hill to reach camp."

Many words have several different meanings; the context indicates which one is intended. *Get*, for example, has over seventy meanings in English; some of them are clear from these sentences:

1. It really *gets* me when he giggles like that.
2. Please *get* some sleep tonight.
3. The bullet *got* him in the belly.
4. When she goes to a party, she *gets* intoxicated.

See also VOCABULARY; DICTIONARIES, C.

contractions   see APOSTROPHES.

conventions of English

ifyoufindthisparagraphhardtoreaditsbecauseithasabs olutelynopunctuationthatmeansnoeasywaytotellwhereo

---

If you find this paragraph hard to read, it's because it has absolutely no punctuation. That means no easy way to tell where one word ends and the next word begins, no easy way to tell where the sentences end and begin, no easy way to tell whether a sentence is a question or a statement. It is hard to get sense out of the letters, isn't it?

Now we add misspelling to the problem. The misspelling is perfectly logical from a phonetic point of view but doesn't agree with the system you're used to. This makes it even harder to get the sense from the words.

C

newordendsandthenextwordbeginsnoeasywaytotellwher
ethesentencesendandbeginnoeasywaytotellwhetherasen
tenceisaquestionorastatementitishardtogetsenseoutofthe
lettersisntit

naoweadmispelengtwothuhprobblumthamispelleeniz
purrfuktleelodgacculfrummafoanettikpoytavyoobuttduz
zntuhgreawiththsistmyureyoostewthissmaykesitevunho
rrdurtoogettthcencefrummthuwurdz

If you can't read the two paragraphs above, look
on page 23 for a translation into conventional English.

The paragraphs show that our language needs the
conventions of

> word division
> punctuation
> capitalization, and
> spelling

to make it easier to extract the sense from the writing.

Learn the conventions of English—*these agreements
among literate people about how to write our language*
—for three reasons:

1. so that you can write more clearly and make
   yourself understood;
2. so that people who read what you write will
   not consider you ignorant; and
3. so that you can read accurately and easily the
   writing of others.

Once you have learned the conventions, you may
want to break them on occasion, but you should break
them only for good reasons, *knowing what you are
doing* and to achieve some special effect, not out of
ignorance.

The conventions of punctuation are given in this
book under the names of the punctuation marks
(COMMAS, PERIODS, QUESTION MARKS, and so on); the
conventions for CAPITALIZATION, DIALOGUE (conversation), and SPELLING occur in the regular alphabetical
listing.

conversation   see DIALOGUE.

coordinating conjunctions   see CONJUNCTION.

correction symbols   see SYMBOLS TO GUIDE
REVISION OF PAPERS.

characterization,

a   the reader

C

dangling participial phrases

Dangling participial phrases are phrases beginning with a participle that do not clearly and sensibly modify a word in a sentence. Correctly used, participial phrases immediately precede or follow the word they modify.

Examples:
1. Wrong

Riding along with his eyes closed, a truck hit the boy.
(dangling participial phrase)

Corrected

Riding along with his eyes closed, the boy was hit by a truck.

2. Wrong

Lying on the beach, the sun burned me badly.
(dangling participial phrase)

Corrected

Lying on the beach, I was burned by the sun.
See also MODIFIERS, PARTICIPLES, PHRASE.

dashes (—)

A dash is a longer line than a HYPHEN. In typing, it is indicated by two hyphen marks: --.

D

A. Dashes are used to indicate a major interruption of a sentence.

Examples:

1. All of us kids—the teacher always called us kids—decided to stay at home Tuesday.
2. Then the teacher—but you already know what she did.
3. Clark whispered, "Please get that thing away from—," but Francine stopped him by fainting.

B. Dashes are also used to show that some further explanation is coming.

Example:

Use dashes sparingly—only when you feel that nothing else will work as well.

NOTES:

1. Whether you use dashes, COMMAS, or PARENTHESES to set off an interruption is a matter of taste. The interruption by dashes tends to be loud and strong, the interruption by parentheses to be more of a whispered aside, and the interruption by commas somewhere in between.

Examples:

1. *Gone with the Wind*—how I detested that old movie!—has at last left Cinema II.
2. *Gone with the Wind* (my mother's favorite way to spend a few hours) has at last left Cinema II.
3. *Gone with the Wind*, in case you hadn't heard, has at last left Cinema II.

2. Either a dash or a COLON can be used to indicate that something more is coming. In this case a dash is usually less strong and definite than a colon—a kind of continuation or afterthought.

Example:

A colon—well, see how it is used on page 19.

See also PARENTHESES, 2.

D

dates

In writing dates, each item after the first one is set off by commas (but there is no comma between the name of the month and the number of the day).

Examples:
1. Today is Wednesday, January 14, 1976.
2. On September 16, 1988, Flo expects to fly to the moon.

Exception:
No comma is used between the month and the year or after the year when the day is omitted.

Example:
They married in June 1930 and have been squabbling ever since.

debating

A debate is a formal contest in argumentation between two individuals or teams, each taking opposite sides of a well-defined question. It is different from a discussion in that the object of a debate is to win the argument, whereas the object of a discussion is to exchange ideas on a subject. A debate is an exercise in PERSUASION through SPEECH MAKING, and the entries in this book under those two headings will be useful to you as you prepare for a debate.

The subject of a formal debate is stated as a *proposition*, thus:

"Resolved, that the system of grading at Elmquist High School should be abolished and a pass/fail system established"; or

"Resolved, that smoking should be prohibited by law to anyone under twenty-five years of age."

In setting up a debate it is important to choose a proposition that provokes an interesting and lively discussion. A good proposition should be debatable, that is, not obviously true or false, limited enough in scope so that the main elements of it can be dealt with in the length of time available, and appropriate to the knowledge and experience of the debaters and the audience. For example, the two propositions given above would probably work well for intelligent junior high, senior high, or college debaters, whereas propositions like "Resolved, that God exists"; or "Resolved, that motherhood is more important than fatherhood" are too vague, broad, and unprovable to be satisfactory.

In preparing for a debate, each side (made up of one, two, or three members) should first of all try to find all the issues on which there may be a clash of opinion and to list arguments, pro and con, probably in two columns. Once the issues are determined, each side assembles its arguments in as convincing a way as possible.

The side that defends the proposition is the *affirmative*; that which opposes the proposition is the *negative*. There are various ways a debate can be conducted. The most common is to have two speakers on each side and to program the speeches thus:

Principal speeches (five minutes each)
1. first affirmative
2. first negative
3. second affirmative
4. second negative

Rebuttal speeches (two minutes each)
1. first negative
2. first affirmative

The *principal* speeches (sometimes called the *constructive* speeches) are prepared in advance and present the main arguments. The *rebuttal* speeches are not prepared exactly in advance but give each side a chance to rebut, that is, to answer, disprove and refute the arguments of the other side. Sometimes a rebuttal speech may end in a brief summary or restatement of the side being defended.

The speeches are strictly timed; a speaker must stop at the end of his or her time, finished or not.

Since a debate is a contest, it is customary to have one or more judges listen to the speakers and then render a decision on which side has done the better job of presenting a convincing argument. The judges may be specialists in the subject being debated, members of the class or group before which the debate is taking place, or members of the faculty. The decision depends on the skills of persuasion demonstrated by each team, not on the basis of the affirmative or negative convictions of the judges.

One danger in debating is that each side may be so anxious to win that it distorts the truth or fails to become familiar with the arguments on both sides. To avoid this danger do not let each team know whether it will be defending the affirmative or negative side of the proposition until shortly before the debate starts, so that each team will be forced to become familiar with the evidence on both sides.

dependent clauses   see CLAUSES.

determiners

Determiners are words that act as NOUN markers. They indicate that a noun will follow. *The* is the most common determiner, and any word that can be replaced by *the* and still make a sensible sentence is likely to be a determiner: "*the* boys," "*those* boys," "*five* boys," "*several* boys." This definition does not apply to ordinary descriptive ADJECTIVES—such as *big* boy, *stupid* boys. In the following sentence the determiners are italicized.

"*Those* little cracks in *the* sidewalk hurt *her* feet and ruined *a* nice day." ARTICLES are always used as determiners.

dewey decimal system   see LIBRARIES, A1.

diacritical marks   see DICTIONARIES, E.

diagraming sentences

Diagraming is a method for showing with hori-

D

zontal, vertical, and slanting lines how the various parts of a sentence relate to each other.

Example:

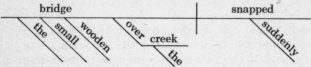

Some students enjoy sentence diagraming, and the practice may help their writing style. More often, however, the activity does not lead to much improvement in people's writing or reading ability. The time is probably better spent in writing and discussing and then revising the writing. Nevertheless, if you want to learn to diagram sentences, you will find the method explained in any traditional grammar.

dialogue

A good way to make SHORT STORIES and other narrative writing interesting and to reveal the personalities of the character is to write dialogue—that is, to set down the words the characters speak. There are specific rules for the punctuation and capitalization of dialogue.

1. Enclose in quotation marks the words actually spoken.

Example:

"That's an explosion," Mary remarked.

2. Use a comma to separate the words spoken from the words that tell who spoke them (except where another form of punctuation is called for; see below).

Examples:

1. "Well, keep calm," George said.
2. Oscar shouted, "Why should I?"

3. Capitalize the first word spoken.

Example:

Mary whispered, "We're all trying to be calm."

4. If the spoken words are an exclamation or a

question, use an exclamation point or a question mark at the end of the quoted words instead of a comma.

Examples:

1. "Be quiet, you wretch!" the man shouted.
2. "Why do we have to be quiet?" asked Karen.

5. If a sentence of dialogue is divided into two parts by such words as *he said* or *she complained*, the second part of the quotation begins with a lower-case letter because it is still the same sentence.

Example:

"Doing exercises," said Gloria, "is my favorite form of torture."

6. If the second part of the quotation is a new sentence, it begins with a capital letter preceded by a period.

Example:

"I'm not educating myself to earn a living," Lincoln said. "No, I'm trying to learn what to do with a living if I ever earn it."

7. If more than one sentence is spoken, do not close the quote until the speaker has finished.

Example:

When asked if he had ever been kicked by a certain mule, the driver replied, "No, sir, he's never kicked me yet. However, sir, he frequently kicks the place where I recently was."

8. Generally, the quotation marks *follow* any other punctuation.

Examples:

1. "Look at my dress," Mary said.
2. His grandmother snarled, "You go wash out your mouth with soap."
3. He constantly used the expression "copasetic."
   NOTE: Cases in which a statement is quoted within a question are an exception.
   Example:
   Did Maud actually say, "I refuse to punctuate"?

D

9. Use single quotation marks to indicate a quotation within a quotation.

Example:

Mr. Jackson explained, "It was Patrick Henry who said, 'Give me liberty or give me death!' "

10. In writing dialogue (conversation), begin a new paragraph whenever the speaker changes, even if only one word is spoken. But be sure that the quotation and such phrases as "he said" are in the same paragraph. Consult a number of novels to learn how it is handled in professional writing and publishing.

11. In real life people often speak in incomplete sentences. This informality may be reflected in written dialogue.

Example:

"Where did you get that crazy hat?" asked Zack.

"From the gutter," Solomon replied.

"From the gutter?" asked Zack.

"Yes, Zack, from the gutter, the good old friendly gutter where I also got my socks," Solomon said.

12. People also tend to interrupt each other in conversations. Interruptions are indicated by a DASH: —.

Example:

"You say you got your socks from—" Zack started to ask.

"Yes, that's what I said," Solomon shouted.

NOTES:

1. Do not use quotation marks to enclose an *indirect* quotation—that is, when you are not quoting a person's words directly.

   Examples:

   Indirect. H. L. Mencken wrote that Puritanism is the lurking fear that someone somewhere is happy.

   Direct. H. L. Mencken wrote, "Puritanism is the lurking fear that someone somewhere is happy."

2. Dialogue is also a major part of writing PLAYS.

dictionaries

Every household should contain a good, recently published dictionary. There are inexpensive paperback dictionaries, which can easily be carried back and forth to school; at home, a so-called college or collegiate abridged dictionary, containing about 150,000 definitions, is most useful. For people with a particular interest in language, an unabridged dictionary, containing from 250,000 to 500,000 definitions, can be helpful.

Each dictionary gives complete instructions for its own use and has a table of contents to show what the book contains in addition to the main section (appendices listing common abbreviations, sections on grammatical rules, and the like).

Here are some facts about the content and organization of dictionaries.

A. *Alphabetical order*

The words defined in the dictionary always appear in alphabetical order: *pouch, poultice, poultry, pounce, pound, pour.* Note that you have to read to the fourth or fifth letter to find each of these words, since they all begin with *pou-*, two begin with *poul-*, and two with *poun-*.

B. *Guide words*

At the top of each page of a dictionary, printed in heavy type, are *guide words*, or running heads. The first of these is the first word on the page, and the second is the last. All the other words on the page come alphabetically between the guide words.

C. *Definition*

Dictionaries list all the major definitions of a word. Many of them do so *chronologically*—that is, they give the *earliest* meaning attributed to a word first. Others arrange meanings by *frequency*—that is, the most *common* meaning is given first. The dictionary's preface generally tells which practice has been followed. In order to find the correct definition you are looking for, you must have some idea of the CONTEXT

D

in which the word is employed. For example, the word *fair* can mean beautiful (a *fair* maiden); clean, spotless, without error (a *fair* copy); light in color, blond (*fair* skin); clear (*fair* weather); just and honest (a *fair* price; *fair* play); and so on.

D. *Parts of speech*

Many words can be used as different PARTS OF SPEECH. To get the meaning you want, consult the part-of-speech labels in the dictionary: *n.* = noun; *pron.* = pronoun; *v.* (or *v.i* and *v.t.*) = verb; *adj.* = adjective; *adv.* = adverb; *prep.* = preposition; *conj.* = conjunction; and *interj.* = interjection.

> *Example:*
> **open,** *adj.* 1. not closed. 2. spread out. 3. available.
> *v.* 1. to make open. 2. to spread out. 3. to start operating.

For major words and in the case of words that are spelled the same but have two distinct meanings (as *bear*, the animal, and *bear*, the verb meaning "support, carry"), two separate entries are generally used.

E. *Pronunciation*

The dictionary gives the pronunciation of words, usually in parentheses after the main entry: **op·pose** (ə pōz′). The mark ′ shows that the accent is on the syllable *pose*; the line over the *o* is called a *macron* (mā′kron) and means that the *o* is sounded long—is pronounced like itself. Another very common mark of pronunciation is the *schwa* (ə) (see *oppose* above). It represents an unaccented sound "uh," as *a* in *ago*, *e* in *agent*, or *i* in *pencil*. These pronunciation indicators are called *diacritical marks*. Most dictionaries give a key to pronunciation at the bottom of every other page.

F. *Usage*

Most dictionaries precede the definition of some words by a word or phrase to indicate that the word is used only under special circumstances. Some terms or spellings, for example, are common in Great Britain but not in the United States; for those, the dictionary will note "chiefly Brit." or "Brit."

Example:

pet·rol ... *n* ... *Brit* : gasoline.

Other such labels may include *arch.* (archaic—that is, old-fashioned and now rarely used), *obsolete* (no longer used, out of date), *slang, var.* (variant), *obsc.* (obscene), *subst.* (substandard), and *dial.* (dialect, usually with a geographical designation, as *dial. New England*).

G. *Spelling*

The dictionary shows how to spell a word and sometimes gives alternative spellings.

Example:

judgment (sometimes also *judgement*).

It also shows how to divide the word into syllables, information which you need when breaking a word at the end of a line.

Example:

op·po·si·tion

H. *Word derivation*

Either preceding or following the definitions of a word, most dictionaries include a note on the word's etymology—its derivation from other languages or earlier forms of the English language. These word derivations are generally enclosed in brackets ([ ]) and use an arrow or the symbol > to show sequence. Abbreviations for other languages are generally explained in the preface.

> NOTE: Knowing the derivation of a word may help to clarify a word's current meaning by showing how it has been used in past times and other places, but it will seldom tell exactly what it means today.

I. *Synonyms and antonyms*

Larger dictionaries often follow the definition of common words by a discussion of their *synonyms* (words having nearly the same meaning) and *antonyms* (words having the opposite meaning).

D

Example:

prejudice . . . Syn. (noun) bias, partiality, pre-possession.

For a more complete set of synonyms, refer to a THESAURUS.

Because different dictionaries use different styles and systems, it is essential to read the explanations at the front of the particular work to understand its organization and symbols.

direct address   see COMMAS, E.

direct objects

The direct object is a word in a sentence that receives the action of the VERB.

Examples:

1. George   hit   the   *tree.*
   (verb)   (direct object)

2. Mary   flattered   *him.*
   (verb)   (direct object)

3. Please   take   those ugly   *pictures*   down.
   (verb)   (direct object)

drama   see PLAYS.

Dialogue, Conversation between characters in a short story, novel, poem, or work of nonfiction. Dialogue may be used to provide background information, to relation- ships or to Advance a story

38

editing   see REVISION OF PAPERS; PROOFREADING.

envelopes   see LETTERS.

essays

For the purpose of this discussion, I define *essay* as an organized paper of moderate length dealing with a specific subject. It is not a SHORT STORY, which is fiction, nor is it a REPORT, which is primarily an organized presentation of information. *Composition* is another word with almost the same meaning as *essay*.

In writing an essay, never lose sight of the PURPOSE of your paper. Why are you writing it, and for whom? Also consider the *material* you will use.

A. *Purpose*

Your *purpose* may be to entertain your reader, to give him information, to persuade him of some point of view (see PERSUASION), to reassure him, to move him to action, or a combination of these. It will help to think about what you are trying to achieve before starting to figure out how to go about the writing.

B. *Material*

Your material may consist of opinions and information you already have in your head; don't overlook that source. Or it may be made up of notes you have taken on reading you have done (see NOTE-TAKING), interviews or conversations you have had, or matters you have heard or seen on TV, on radio, or at the movies. Whatever the material, unless you have an amazingly well-organized and retentive mind, you will probably do a better job if you spend a little time arranging your material in some way before you start writing. Of course once you start to write, you will probably find that your arrangement needs some rearranging as you go. It is rarely possible simply to follow an OUTLINE in writing a full essay. Most writers find that the writing itself forces them to reshape the organization as they proceed. But having an outline or plan before they start helps avoid some pain and saves time later on.

C. *Organization: beginning, middle, end*

Most instruction on organizing a piece of writing tells the student that his paper should have a beginning, a middle, and an end. It is obvious that you have to start a subject and you have to finish; what comes in between is the middle. But usually it is not as cut and dried as the old country preacher's formula for a good sermon—"First you tell 'em what you're going to tell 'em; then you tell 'em; then you tell 'em what you told 'em"—or as the King's directions to the White Rabbit in presenting evidence at the trial of the Knave in *Alice in Wonderland*: "Begin at the beginning, and go on until you come to the end: then stop." Still, you could do worse.

1. *Beginning* You do need to give some thought to the way to start your paper. Sometimes the beginning is the hardest part, and it may be better to try to write the middle first, deciding later on the best way to begin. One good way to begin a paper is with a *question*: "Why should students be required to attend classes when they are likely to learn more by staying out in the real world?" Or "What kind of knowledge of sex and love is a fifteen-year-old kid likely to pick up if he's never read a book on the subject?"

Another way is to begin with a *statement*: "If you make your eyes really see and your ears really hear, you can figure out a lot about a neighborhood by just sitting for an hour on the front steps." Or "After talking with five teachers and ten students in my class, I believe there are three changes we ought to make at

E

this school next year, and I intend to see that they are made."

Don't turn your reader off by writing, "This is going to be a paper about . . ." or "I've been given the topic *fish* to write about, and . . ."

2. *Middle* You may want to start your paper right in the middle of the subject. In no case should you wait too long to get to the real heart of the paper. The middle really constitutes the substance of what you have to say. It will be the longest part of the paper, the part that needs the most careful organizing and arranging.

A good way to organize ideas and information for a paper is to *list the main ideas*, following each with the points you might use to develop it: facts, examples, incidents, anecdotes, reasons, and explanations. If your subject is at all complicated, you will have to make such a listing in order to avoid getting confused.

While many people do not find it necessary, or even helpful, to follow a formal outline strictly, others do find such an outline useful (see OUTLINING). If you do use an outline, think of it as a tool to serve you, not as a form that will dominate you.

3. *End* A good piece of writing ends in such a way that the reader has a satisfying feeling that the work is finished. Of course he doesn't want to read some such phrasing as "And so I have shown that . . ." or "Now I bring my paper to a conclusion." But he does want to have a sense of completion. This ending can be another question arising from the material in the paper: "I've decided what I'm going to do about [whatever it is], but what are you going to do?" or "What have you seen in the past week that could prove me wrong?"

The ending can also consist of a vigorous restatement of the main idea of the paper: "It is true that in the real world out there we have crime, love, and action. We also have the vivid world of TV and the movies. But unless we can bring these realities into the schools where through discussion and reading we can give some shape to them in our minds, we are more likely to end up confused than educated." Or "So it's not a matter of whether or not there will be sex education for fifteen-year-olds, but rather what kind of sex education there will be. Only the school with a free atmosphere, good teachers, and plenty of discussion is qualified to give the best kind."

D. *Paragraphing*

I feel that much of the instruction given under the heading "How to Write a Paragraph" is not very useful or realistic. It leads the student to suppose that real people organize their writing by thinking of topic sentences, by supporting the topic sentences with a few points, and by going on gracefully to the next topic sentence, supporting points, and so on, until the end. I don't know any professional writer who works that way.

And yet paragraphing is important. For one thing, the reader gets tired and discouraged looking at a page of writing or print that goes on and on with never a break. A reader needs to be helped along by some signs of how the ideas in the paper are progressing. He wants to be allowed to take a mental breath now and then before plunging back into the argument. Thus, you will make your readers happier and get your ideas across better if you write in PARAGRAPHS.

The main points and subpoints in the outline or arrangement of ideas that you may have made before starting to write will probably, for the most part, turn out to be paragraphs in your paper (see also TRANSITIONS). When you have finished the *first draft* of a paper (see REVISION OF PAPERS), you will do well to look it over to check whether you have paragraphed it in a way that will be most helpful to your readers. In your first draft you can indicate that you want a new paragraph by using the sign ¶.

These suggestions should help in taking hold of any topic, idea or assignment and coping with it adequately. As you become experienced in writing essays, you will

E

discover ways that especially suit your style. The suggestions will also help you organize your thinking and the information you have collected. No set of devices, however, can do your thinking or provide material for you.

For suggestions about how to do a first and final draft and on PROOFREADING, see REVISION OF PAPERS. For suggestions on a special kind of writing task, see REPORTS; see also PERSUASION.

"etc."

The abbreviation "etc." should not be used in any writing more formal than a personal LETTER. The expressions "and so on," "and the like," or "and so forth" are preferable, but usually it makes for stronger writing to add one or two more examples and omit "and so on."

> *Example:*
> "A healthful diet includes green vegetables—beans, peas, broccoli, and the like."
>
> NOTE: Following the expressions "including" or "such as," there is no need to add one of these phrases.
> *Example:*
> *Wrong.* "Norman Mailer's works include novels, films, plays, and the like."
> *Correct.* "Norman Mailer's works include novels, films, and plays."

examinations   see TAKING TESTS AND EXAMS and REVIEWING FOR TESTS AND EXAMS.

exclamation points (!)

An exclamation point indicates the end of an exclamation—a statement or utterance expressing strong emphasis or emotion. Sentences that end in an exclamation point are called *exclamatory sentences.*

> *Examples:*
> 1. Come here this instant! [emphasis]

2. The dogs are attacking the rabbits again!
   [emotion]
3. Hurray! Wow! Heavens! Help! [emotion]
   NOTES:
   1. Use an exclamation point in sentences that
      are not questions but begin with *what*,
      why, or *how*.
      Examples:
      1. What a fine day!
      2. How bored I am!
   2. Never use more than one exclamation
      point unless you are writing comic strips.
      In general use the exclamation point spar-
      ingly. If in doubt, leave it out.

_____

_____

_____

_____

_____

_____

_____

_____

_____

_____

_____

E

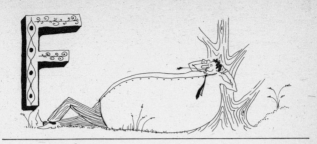

figurative language

Figurative language in speech and writing involves using comparisons—figures of speech. The two most common figures of speech are *metaphors* and *similes*. The opposite of figurative language is literal language.

Examples:

1. *literal.*   The eagle holds on to the crag with his claws, high up in the lonely blue spaces of air on a sunny day.

   figurative.   "He clasps the crag with crooked hands,
   Close to the sun in azure lands."
   —ALFRED TENNYSON

2. *literal.*   His dreams were small, pleasant and disorganized.

   figurative.   "His dreams were light as feathers, and blew this way and that."
   —JOHN UPDIKE

In the first example the eagle doesn't literally have crooked hands, but that is what they remind Tennyson of; nor are the great spaces of blue sky "azure lands," but calling them that strikes the reader. The user of figurative language sees one thing in terms of another; he employs an enlightening, impressive sort of double vision. Updike sees dreams as feathers and their lack of organization as a random drift.

Two commonly distinguished figures of speech are *similes* and *metaphors*.

A. *Similes*

F

A simile expresses comparison using *like* or *as*.

Examples:

1. "The pigeons are *pompous as bankers*."

    —Phyllis McGinley

2. "Ali drove a right *straight as a pole* into the stunned center of Foreman's head."

    —Norman Mailer

3. "Dawn comes up *like thunder* out of China 'crost the bay!" —Rudyard Kipling

4. "The exhausted light [from the fireplace] beat up and down the wall . . . *like a bird trying to find its way out of the room*." —Eudora Welty

5. "His rosy hands were folded on the shiny desk, reflected *like water flowers*." —John Updike

B. *Metaphors*

A metaphor expresses comparison without the use of *like* or *as*.

Examples:

1. "Wind is a cat that prowls the night."

    —Ethel Romig Fuller

2. "Life's but a walking shadow . . . , a tale told by an idiot . . ." —William Shakespeare

3. "Suddenly Ali hit him again. . . . The sound of a bat thunking into a watermelon was heard around the ring." —Norman Mailer

4. Lincoln's "thoughts were roots that firmly grasped the granite truth."

    —Edwin Markham

5. "Hunger is the best of cooks."

    —German Proverb

In writing, use similes and metaphors not as ornaments but as ways to make your reader see and feel what you want him to or to express the way you see and feel.

Be careful not to use *mixed metaphors*, in which the comparison changes form, unless you are trying to be funny.

Examples:

1. When we first met, he bristled like a porcu-

pine, but as we talked he began to thaw. [The comparison changes from porcupine to ice.]

2. He's a big wheel on the student council, but he doesn't know which end is up. [Wheels don't have ends, nor do they think about them.]
3. She's the mainspring of the speech team and really bowls them over in a debate. [The comparison changes from a spring to a bowling ball.]
4. The American eagle will never turn tail and run. [An eagle doesn't run or turn tail like a rabbit or deer.]

When you read, try to recognize when the writer is using figurative language. Otherwise, you may miss much of the meaning. The following poem by Robert Frost is a good example of metaphorical writing. Frost said, "Poetry is a way of saying something while saying something else."

The Road Not Taken

Two roads diverged in a yellow wood,
And sorry I could not travel both
And be one traveler, long I stood
And looked down one as far as I could
To where it bent in the undergrowth;

Then took the other, as just as fair,
And having perhaps the better claim,
Because it was grassy and wanted wear;
Though as for that, the passing there
Had worn them really about the same,

And both that morning equally lay
In leaves no step had trodden black.
Oh, I kept the first for another day!
Yet knowing how way leads on to way,
I doubted if I should ever come back.

I shall be telling this with a sigh
Somewhere ages and ages hence:

F

Two roads diverged in a wood, and I—
I took the one less traveled by,
And that has made all the difference.

C. *Other common figures of speech*
Apostrophe

An apostrophe is a figure of speech in which the writer or speaker directly addresses an object that cannot understand, as in Edna St. Vincent Millay's poem "God's World":

"O World, I cannot hold thee close enough!"

> NOTE: *Apostrophe* the figure of speech is entirely different from APOSTROPHE the punctuation mark.

Hyperbole

Hyperbole is exaggeration for special effect, as when Shakespeare's Lady Macbeth looks at her hand that helped Macbeth murder King Duncan and says, "All the perfumes of Arabia will not sweeten this little hand."

Irony

To use irony is to say something but mean the opposite, usually in a bitter or humorous manner, as when a coach says to the outfielder who just dropped an easy fly, "That was a great play," or the British soldier-poet Siegfried Sassoon writes:

"Does it matter?—losing your sight? . . .
There's such splendid work for the blind."

Personification

Personification is treating an inanimate thing or idea as if it were a person, or treating oneself as an inanimate object or idea.

Examples:

1. The floods clap their hands. —JOHN MILTON
2. I am a copper wire slung in the air,
   Slim against the sun I make not even a clear
   line of shadow. —CARL SANDBURG

figures of speech   see FIGURATIVE LANGUAGE.

final consonants   see SPELLING RULES.

final drafts   see REVISION OF PAPERS.

first drafts   see REVISION OF PAPERS.

footnotes

When you cite a source in writing a formal paper, either quoting the expert's exact words or giving a summary of the author's ideas, identify the source by a *footnote* at the bottom of the page. Each footnote in the paper should be numbered in sequence, starting with the number 1. Place the number, raised a little above the line, at the end of the quotation or reference in the text; place the same number in front of the footnote that appears at the end of the page.

The purpose of footnotes is to tell the reader exactly where your information comes from in case he wants to check or to read more, and also to give him an indication of how reliable your paper is.

There are a number of styles for writing footnotes; I give the most commonly used one here. *Major items of information in a footnote are separated by commas, and the footnote should contain: (1) the author's name, first name or initials first; (2) the title of the work cited—use quotation marks for an article or chapter title; underline (italicize) the name of a magazine or title of a book; (3) for books, the place of publication and the name of the publisher in parentheses; (4) the number of the volume (if there are two or more); (5) date of the publication; and (6) page number(s).*

    Examples:

Book   Isser Harel, *The House on Garibaldi Street*, New York (The Viking Press), 1975, pp. 73–76.

Magazine   Isaac Asimov, "Clippings from Tomorrow's Newspapers, News Stories of
2024," *Saturday Review*, August 24,
1974, pp. 78–81.[1]

Footnotes may also be used to give additional
information or explanation that might interrupt the
text. Note the examples used to augment this article.
If there are only a few footnotes and not more than one
per page, you may use an asterisk (*) instead of a
number.

If you use the same reference more than once,
abbreviate the reference after the first full citation:

Examples:

1. If citing the title in the footnote directly
   before, either, "Harel, pp. 92–93" or, *"ibid.,*[2]
   pp. 92–93."
2. If citing a title referred to again after other
   footnotes have intervened, either, "Asimov,
   op. cit.,[3] p. 82" or, "Asimov, p. 82."

   NOTES:
   1. Some teachers and publishers insist on a
      particular style in footnotes. Since there
      are several acceptable ways, be sure you
      find out exactly what style is expected
      before you work up your final draft.
   2. While footnotes may make your paper look
      scholarly, they can also render it ponder-
      ous and harder to read. Use footnotes
      sparingly, especially if you are not prepar-
      ing a scholarly report.

form for papers

Whenever you work on a paper as an assignment
for a teacher, be sure you know what form the teacher

---

[1]Note that the most common form used in a footnote is
slightly different from that used in listing a source in a
BIBLIOGRAPHY.

[2]*ibid.,* from the Latin *ibidem,* meaning "in the same
place."

[3]*op. cit.,* from the Latin *opera citato,* meaning "in the
work cited."

wishes you to use. You may feel that the teacher is excessively fussy to insist on a particular form. In fact, the teacher's job of reading and commenting on a mass of papers is made easier if they all are in the same form, and it's no more work for you. If no form is prescribed, a convenient one is the following:

	Name	Date	Grade & Section
← 1½″ → (margin to allow for comments and corrections)		Title or Label	
		[skip a line]	
	This is the beginning of the		

fragments   see SENTENCE FRAGMENTS; SENTENCES.

frame tests

A frame test is a sentence made up especially for the purpose of testing out to what PART OF SPEECH words belong. It has a blank in it in which only one part of speech or word class will fit sensibly. If you need to know whether a word can be used as a NOUN, VERB, LINKING VERB, ADJECTIVE, ADVERB, or PREPOSITION, try it out in the frame tests. Frame tests do not always work, but they are often helpful in giving you a sense of the function of words. The most useful frame tests follow.

Noun: I am happy about (the) _____.
(noun)

Verb: Let's _____ (it).
(verb)

(Such endings of verbs as *-ing* or *-ed* must be removed to make the frame test work.)

Linking verb: They _____ nice.
(linking verb)

F

Adjective: The thing was very _____.

(adjective)

(The endings *-er* or *-est* must be removed from the adjective to make the frame test work.)

Adverb: Either: He said it _____ or: He _____

(adverb)   (adverb)

said it.

Preposition: It went _____ the thing(s).

(preposition)

(This frame test will not work for the very common preposition *of.*)

friendly letters   see LETTERS, A.

Foreshadowing; an author's use of hints or clues about events which will occur later in a narrative.

Flashback, an interruption in the action of a story, play, or work of nonfiction to show an episode that happened at Provide. background information necessary to an understanding of the characters or the plot.

54

gerund phrases

A gerund phrase is a phrase containing a GERUND. A gerund phrase is used as a NOUN.

Examples:

1. *His habitual snoring* slowly drove me wild.
2. After a vacation, I hate *arriving at home.*
3. Beneath *the roaring of traffic* men were silently conspiring.

gerunds

A gerund is a form of a VERB used like a NOUN. Like a noun, it can be used as SUBJECT, COMPLEMENT or OBJECT.

Examples:

1. *Giggling* is a form of nervousness. [subject]
2. His worst habit is loud *giggling.* [complement]
3. Mr. Jacob's frankness stopped our *giggling.* [direct object]
4. She fell asleep during the *giggling.* [object of preposition]

NOTE: Gerunds end in *-ing.* They are not to be confused with PARTICIPLES, many of which also end in *-ing.*

grades   see MARKS.

grammar

Most of our speaking, READING, and writing is made up of SENTENCES. These, in turn, are made up of various parts, or elements. There are bad sentences and good sentences, ugly sentences and graceful sentences, correct sentences and incorrect sentences. The rules about sentences and how they are made are called grammar. It is not necessary to learn grammar from books in order to read and write well, though it may help. In fact, as soon as you learned to speak a language, you knew, by imitation, how to talk grammatically. What you spoke was the grammar of English, or Spanish, or some other language. But you couldn't explain or talk about the grammar you knew. You just used it.

A. *Word order*

In English, one of the most important principles of grammar is *word order*. You can see how it works by looking at the following arrangements of exactly the same eight words.

1. Grandmother nice bothers my old dog little that.
2. My bothers old grandmother nice that dog little.
3. My grandmother nice old bothers that dog little.
4. That dog little bothers nice old my grandmother.
5. That little dog bothers my nice old grandmother.
6. That nice old grandmother bothers my little dog.
7. My nice old dog bothers that little grandmother.

Only the last three sentences have real meaning, and that meaning changes depending on the word order.

The *position* of a word, as well as the order, is also important in English. Note, for example, what happens as the word *only* moves along this sentence:

Only he kissed the girl yesterday.
He only kissed the girl yesterday.
He kissed only the girl yesterday.

He kissed the only girl yesterday.
He kissed the girl only yesterday.
He kissed the girl yesterday only.

B. *Inflection*

Another principle of grammar, less important in English than in many other languages, is *inflection*—changes in the form of words and in their endings. The most important inflectional changes in modern English are endings, mainly *s* and *es* to show plurals in NOUNS; *'s* to show POSSESSION in nouns; *ed, en, s,* and *ing* to show changes of TENSE in VERBS; and *ly, er,* and *est* to show COMPARISON in ADVERBS and ADJECTIVES. PRONOUNS change form rather than ending: *he, his, him; she, hers, her; I, mine, my, me;* and so on.

C. *Usage*

Another kind of grammar is called *usage*—the study of what is correct and incorrect, acceptable and unacceptable. A sentence such as *He don't allow nobody to do nothing where he live at* makes its meaning perfectly clear; in a sense, therefore, it is a grammatical English sentence. But the usage is not acceptable as *standard English.* It is *nonstandard.* For many people, speaking and writing standard, "correct" English is important, and anyone who deviates from standard usage risks being thought ignorant, crude, uneducated, or amusing. In a situation where you want to avoid giving such an impression, it is helpful to use standard English.

Certain ways of speaking and writing are *appropriate* to some situations and inappropriate to others. You probably speak differently to your old aunt than you do to your best friend; you use different styles of writing in a formal report and in a quick note to a classmate. On a camping trip, when you are ready for sleep, you might say, "I'm going to sack out." In the unlikely event that you are the houseguest of royalty, on the other hand, you might say, "I should like to retire." Neither expression is wrong, but either would be ridiculous in the inappropriate situation.

> If that thou wilt speak aright
> Six things thou must observe then:
> What thou speakest, and of what wight [person or creature],
> Where, to whom, why, and when.
> —ANONYMOUS, c. 1530

See also LANGUAGE and SENTENCES.

_____

_____

_____

_____

_____

_____

_____

_____

_____

_____

_____

helping verbs   see VERBS, C.

homework   see STUDY SKILLS.

hyperboles   see FIGURATIVE LANGAUGE.

hyphens (-)
A hyphen is used either to show where words are divided or to indicate the joining of two closely related words.
1. Use a hyphen to divide a word at the end of a line, between syllables (see SYLLABICATION). If you do not know where to make the division, refer to a DICTIONARY. *Never* divide a one-syllable word.
   Examples:
   1. Please do not inter-
      rupt while I sing.
   2. The little child was cry-
      ing buckets of tears.
      NOTES:
      1. Generally, words are divided after a PREFIX (sub-
         conscious),
         before a SUFFIX (cumber- and between
                              some),
         double letters (cin-
                              namon).
      2. Always place the hyphen at the end of the line, never at the beginning of the next.
2. Use a hyphen when writing out numbers under one hundred.

60

Examples:
twenty-five; ninety-nine
3. Use a hyphen to join two words that together modify a NOUN (see MODIFIERS).
   Examples:
   1. a two-thirds majority
   2. a self-sealing bottle
   3. the pine-forested hill
4. Always use a hyphen with such prefixes as *self-*, *ex-*, and *all-*.
   Examples:
   self-employed, ex-president, all-American

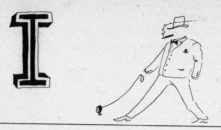

"ie-ei"   see SPELLING RULES, 1.

index   see BOOKS.

indirect objects

The indirect object is a NOUN or PRONOUN in a SENTENCE that tells to *whom* or *what*, or for *whom* or *what*, the action of the VERB is done.

Examples:

1. Lolly gave the   *kid*   a black eye. [to whom]
   (ind. obj.)

2. Thus she earned the   *school*   a bad reputation.
   (ind. obj.)
   [for what]

3. Buy   *me*   a lollipop, Mom. [for whom]
   (ind. obj.)

NOTES:

1. When the words *to* or *for* are used, the words following them are parts of prepositional phrases, rather than indirect objects.
   Examples:
   prepositional phrases. The crowds gave a great ovation *to Lindbergh.*
   Mother cooked some stew *for the family.*
   indirect objects. The crowds gave *Lindbergh* a great ovation.
   Mother cooked the *family* some stew.

2. The indirect object precedes the *direct object.*

3. When you use a pronoun as an indirect object, use its objective form (or CASE)— *me, him, her, them,* and so on.

See also DIRECT OBJECTS.

indirect quotation

An indirect quotation reports what someone said without reproducing the exact words.

Examples:

1. Direct quotation. Elise screamed, "Let me go!"
2. Indirect quotation. Elise screamed that she wanted to be let go.
3. Direct quotation. Gabe grumbled, "Drop dead."
4. Indirect quotation. Gabe grumbled that we should drop dead.

infinitive phrases

An infinitive phrase is a PHRASE containing an infinitive.

Examples:

1. *To refuse to talk with your parents* may cause them to start prying. [as noun]
2. He was delighted *to hide in the woods.* [as adverb]
3. The whole class ran out *to observe the scene.* [as adverb]

infinitives

The infinitive is a verb form with the word *to* before it: "to exaggerate"; "to slather"; "to prove"; "to annoy"; "to trample."

Infinitives can be used as NOUNS, ADJECTIVES or ADVERBS.

Examples:

1. *To laugh* is less creative than *to weep.* [as nouns—subject and complement]
2. The bear decided *to wait* behind the rock. [as noun, object of verb]
3. Meals *to eat* and clothes *to wear* are better than daffodils *to contemplate.* [as adjectives, modifying nouns]
4. Henry's sister hit him *to make* him angry. [as adverb, modifying verb]

I

inflection   see GRAMMAR, B.

intensifiers   see QUALIFIERS.

interjections

An interjection is one of the eight PARTS OF SPEECH in traditional GRAMMAR. It is a word that has little grammatical relation to other words in a sentence, and it often expresses emotion: "Wow!" "Heavens!" "Goodness!" "Whew!"

> *Examples:*
> 1. *My,* you look wretched today!
> 2. *Ouch!* You got me where it hurts!
> 3. *Well,* let's get started.

intransitive verbs   see VERBS.

invitations   see LETTERS.

irregular verbs

An irregular VERB is one that does not form its past or present participle in the regular way.

The regular form is:

present	past	past participle
enjoy	enjoyed	(have) enjoyed
imagine	imagined	(have) imagined

The following are a few common irregular verbs:

present	past	past participle
think	thought	(have) thought
speak	spoke	(have) spoken
know	knew	(have) known
am, are	was, were	(have) been
fall	fell	(have) fallen

If you are not sure how an irregular verb forms its PRINCIPAL PARTS, check the DICTIONARY. Irregular forms will be listed, usually immediately following the entry word and before the definitions.

NOTES:
1. These verbs cause much trouble in English, especially for people who do not have a good ear for language or whose native language is not English.
2. Most long verbs and all verbs that are relatively new to English (such as *rocket*, *contact*, and *brainstorm*) are regular. Little children just learning to speak, with good grammatical logic often make mistakes by using irregular verbs as if they were regular: "I speak; I speaked yesterday; Mama thinks, Mama thinked; she has thinked all day."

italics

Italics are letters that lean to the right *like this*. In typing or handwriting, they are indicated by UNDERLINING.

_____

_____

_____

_____

_____

_____

_____

_____

_____

_____

I

language

Human language is a system of symbols. No other animal has a complex symbolic language that must be learned. Animal language is largely instinctive, while *the basic human language is speech*, which is composed of sounds that symbolize things, ideas, actions, and the like. The word *table*, for example, means a raised slab because we have agreed that it will be the symbol for what we know a table to be. Otherwise, there is nothing at all "tablish" about the sound of the word. Written language uses letters or other signs to stand for the sounds of speech.

We learn to read, often with considerable effort, by noticing or being taught that groups of letters stand for the sounds that we already know how to speak. We learn to write, with even greater effort, by learning to form the letters, which are symbols of sounds, and to put them together on paper so that others can read what we "say."

Since human language is a form of human behavior, there is nothing absolute about it. It has developed slowly throughout human history and will continue to develop. No genuine language ever changes radically or rapidly; it is stable and modifies gradually to meet new tastes and conditions.

In the English language there are perhaps 600,000 words, possibly more, but most of them are known only to specialists and are rarely used. The average mature person has a *use vocabulary* of about 10,000 words and a *recognition* vocabulary of 30,000 to 40,000.

L

New words frequently enter a language from science, slang or invention, from other languages, or because of new conditions and experiences; some old words drop out (become *obsolete* or *archaic*). But the vast bulk of the language remains stable.

In the world there are perhaps 3,000 spoken languages. Only thirteen of them have 50 million speakers or more. Those spoken by the largest number of people are Chinese, English, Hindustani, Spanish, and Russian. English is the language most widely scattered over the world, although Chinese has many more speakers.

See also GRAMMAR.

letters

A. *Friendly letters*

You probably need no help in writing letters to your friends. You either write letters or you don't, and how you write each depends on your relationship with the particular friend. However, there is something to be said for using the conventional form, since it gives your correspondent the information necessary for a reply. One "correct" form is on page 71.

B. *Invitations*

If you are sending invitations to a party or some other event, be sure to include all the vital information: where, when (not only the date but also the day of the week), what time it will begin and end, where and how to reply.

When you receive a social invitation, be sure to answer, and answer promptly. If the invitation includes the letters R.S.V.P. followed by an address, *write* a reply as directed. If R.S.V.P. is followed by a telephone number, a *telephoned* reply is proper. "R.S.V.P." is the conventional way of indicating, "Please reply." It is an abbreviation of the French, *Répondez s'il vous plaît*.

C. *Business letters*

You should be less casual in writing business letters

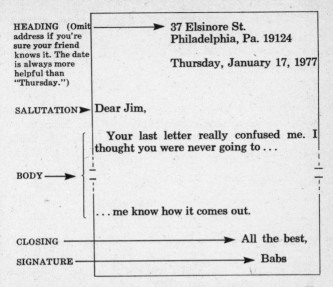

HEADING (Omit address if you're sure your friend knows it. The date is always more helpful than "Thursday.")

37 Elsinore St.
Philadelphia, Pa. 19124

Thursday, January 17, 1977

SALUTATION ▸ Dear Jim,

BODY ⟶
    Your last letter really confused me. I thought you were never going to . . .

. . . me know how it comes out.

CLOSING ⟶ All the best,

SIGNATURE ⟶ Babs

than in correspondence with friends. If you are really serious about the business at hand—applying for a job, making a suggestion, ordering merchandise, getting satisfaction about a complaint, making an appointment to sell goods or services—you are likely to be most successful if you use a correct form, get right to the point, stick to it, and stop when you're done. Otherwise your business reader may judge you unkindly and be less receptive to your purpose. If you can, *type* your letters. In any case, make sure that they are legible. It's a good idea to keep a carbon copy for reference.

The correct form for a business letter is on page 72.

NOTES:
1. If you know the name of the person in the business who will be dealing with your letter, use it:
   "Mr. John G. Masters, Sales Manager
   Dear Mr. Masters:"
2. When placing an order, be sure to give the quantity, color, catalog number, price, and any other vital information to eliminate any possibility of mistake.

L

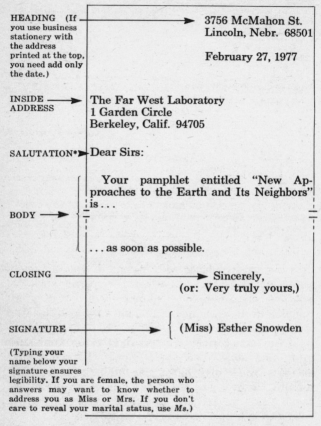

HEADING (If you use business stationery with the address printed at the top, you need add only the date.)

3756 McMahon St.
Lincoln, Nebr. 68501

February 27, 1977

INSIDE ADDRESS

The Far West Laboratory
1 Garden Circle
Berkeley, Calif. 94705

SALUTATION* Dear Sirs:

BODY

Your pamphlet entitled "New Approaches to the Earth and Its Neighbors" is . . .

. . . as soon as possible.

CLOSING

Sincerely,
(or: Very truly yours,)

SIGNATURE

(Miss) Esther Snowden

(Typing your name below your signature ensures legibility. If you are female, the person who answers may want to know whether to address you as Miss or Mrs. If you don't care to reveal your marital status, use *Ms.*)

3. In making a complaint or asking for a refund, keep a friendly tone and explain your reasons clearly. An angry letter rarely

---

salutation: In business, it's still a man's world. Hence the "Sir." In olden days letters were sometimes addressed "Dear Sir or Madam as the case may be." This is ponderous and isn't done any longer. If you don't want to assume that management is masculine, you may write, "Dear Friends."

---

serves its purpose as well as a reasonable one—and the world has enough misery in it anyway.

D. *Envelopes*

What you write on the envelope makes it possible for your letter to reach its destination or, if for some reason it does not, allows it to be returned to you. Therefore, be clear.

Ms. Alicia Link
375 Jacob Ave.
Quakake, Pa. 18245

Mr. Francis Smithers
Sales Manager
The Tryon Hose Company
62 South Smith St.
Manchester, Mo. 63011

It is permissible to put the return address on the back flap of the envelope of a friendly letter, although it makes it a little harder for the post office if they must return the letter to you.

libraries

Libraries are collections of books, periodicals, records, and microfilm arranged so as to make it easy to find what is needed. They come in various sizes and shapes: a classroom library, a bookmobile, a library in a small town, a school library, a vast urban public library, a business library, or the library of a great university. Libraries are inexhaustible sources of information and pleasure. Librarians are always ready to help you make good use of them.

A. *Arrangement of books*

The books in a library are grouped according to subject. Some *fiction*—that is, full-length novels—is arranged alphabetically by author's last name. *Non-*

L

fiction and other fictional forms are arranged by a combination of numbers and letters according to one of two systems.

1. *The Dewey Decimal System* is used in most school and public libraries. It divides all subjects about which books might be written into ten main categories, spanning numbers in the hundreds:

000–099	General works (encyclopedias, newspapers, periodicals)
100–199	Philosophy (conduct, ethics, psychology)
200–299	Religion (Bibles, mythology)
300–399	Social sciences (economics, law, education, government)
400–499	Language (dictionaries, grammars, languages)
500–599	Pure sciences (mathematics, physics, chemistry, astronomy)
600–699	Technology (engineering, radio, television, business, medicine)
700–799	Arts and recreation
800–899	Literature (poems, plays, essays, but *not* other fiction)
900–999	History (history, travel, geography, biography)

Each category is broken down into hundreds of subcategories so that an expert can tell from a book's *call number* quite exactly what it is about.
Example:
923.3H is the call number for *The Age of Moguls* by Stewart Holbrook, a work in in nineteenth-century American history.

2. *The Library of Congress Classification System* is preferred in most college, university and research libraries. In this system, the major subject classes are indicated by letters of the alphabet followed by numbers. In this

system, also, each book has a *call number* by which it can be exactly identified and located on the shelves. The major divisions are as follows:

A   General Works
B   Philosophy—Religion
C   History—Auxiliary Sciences
D   History and Topography (except America)
E–F America
G   Geography—Anthropology
H   Social Sciences
J   Political Science
K   Law
L   Education
M   Music
N   Fine Arts
P   Language and Literature
Q   Science
R   Medicine
S   Agriculture—Plant and Animal Industry
T   Technology
U   Military Science
V   Naval Science
Z   Bibliography and Library Science

B. *How to find a book*

Nearly every library has a *card catalog*, the central file which will allow you to locate any book in the collection. There are generally three cards for each book—an *author* card, a *title* card, and a *subject* card. In most libraries all cards are arranged in the catalog drawers in a single alphabetical order. Below are three cards referring to a book by Murray L. Wax, *Indian Americans, Unity and Diversity*.

The number in the upper left-hand corner of each card is the *call number*.

Many smaller libraries give their users open access to the shelves, so they can find the books they want. In larger libraries, users note on a slip of paper the

L

| 970.5 | Wax, Murray L. |
| W37 | Indian Americans, unity and diversity |

| 970.5 | Indian Americans, unity and |
| W37 | diversity |

Wax, Murray L.
Indian Americans, unity and diversity

| 970.5 | INDIANS, AMERICAN |
| W37 | |

Wax, Murray L.
Indian Americans, unity and diversity
Englewood Cliffs, New Jersey, Prentice-Hall [c1971]
236p. (Ethnic groups in American life series)

INDIANS, AMERICAN
INDIANS, AMERICAN
(SOCIAL CONDITIONS)

call number, author, and title of each book they want and present it to the librarian at the call desk. The book will then be brought to you. In large libraries most of the books are kept in *the stacks*—closely placed shelves not open to the general public.

There is usually a section of the library set aside for *reference books* such as encyclopedias, dictionaries, guides to periodical literature (magazines), and atlases. Most of these may not be taken out, but many libraries provide copying machines so that at small cost you can make a copy of any pages you would like to take with you.

Do not hesitate to ask a librarian how to find a book or how best to use the particular library you are in.

library of congress classification system
see LIBRARIES, A2.

linking verbs see VERBS, B.

_____

_____

_____

_____

_____

_____

_____

_____

_____

_____

_____

_____

_____

_____

_____

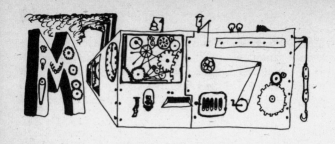

main verbs   see VERBS, C.

marks

Marks or grades should be considered as information, not as coin to be earned. To benefit most from a marking system, try to understand what a mark means; if you don't know, ask. Most schools provide an official description of marks—for example: A, A— = superior; B+ = very good; B = good; B— = fairly good; C+, C = satisfactory; C— = barely satisfactory; D = poor or deficient; and F = failing. Since *failing* is such a serious term (after all, *you* aren't failing; it's just that your effort in a given paper, activity, or course fails to meet the requirements, according to the judgment of the teacher), some schools use NC = no credit; or U = unsatisfactory.

There are other systems: those based on 100 = perfect; those using I, II, and III, and so on, in place of A, B, C, and the like; and those using still other terms or labels. Whatever the system, try to understand it and use it to guide your future efforts. If you get a lower mark than you expected, ask why—not as a complaint, but because you need to know how you fell short in order to do better next time.

A few schools use a simple system of "pass/fail" or "satisfactory/unsatisfactory" and some give no marks at all. Many student and teachers, especially in upper grades, have found such systems too indefinite to suit them.

Often a comment accompanies the mark. Whereas it is only natural for most people to zero in on the mark

("Whadja get?")—and the mark does give an unsentimental, brief indication of where you stand in relation to the standards of the school or class—the comment is much more informative and deserves your careful attention. It should guide your efforts to improve your performance, if you need to. If you don't know how to do better, ask.

Also, remember that in any group half the members are average and below, half are average and above—and usually the average mark (or the median or middle mark) is in the *B*'s, not the *C*'s. You should therefore not feel discouraged if you are not above average. High marks are pleasant to get, and they may help you to get to the next level of your education, but much more important is what and how well you learn; quite often a mark cannot reflect that value accurately.

On English papers, you may receive several marks —one for content, one for spelling, one for mechanics (punctuation and capitalization). Be sure you know what they mean. Also be sure you understand and benefit from the comments and SYMBOLS TO GUIDE REVISION OF PAPERS. Try not to make the same mistake more than once.

material   see ESSAYS.

mechanics of English   see CONVENTIONS OF ENGLISH.

memorization

Some people memorize and retain materials easily; some have great difficulty. A good memory is a real advantage, but it is not by any means the most important part of intelligence. Be thankful if you have, or can develop, a good memory; but do not despair if your memory is poor. You can always look things up.

What follows is a method for memorizing poetry or prose that works well for many people, although not for all. Try these steps if you are not successful with your present method.

M

1. Read the passage through aloud, and make sure you understand it.
2. Read it again aloud three or four times, with full expression.
3. Close your eyes and see how far you can go in saying the passage. When you're stuck, open your eyes and refresh your memory. Proceed thus to the end.
4. Now memorize a short section at a time. Read the lines; close your eyes and say the lines.
5. Try the entire passage with a partner to prompt you when you get stuck. If you can't get a prompter, help yourself out by glancing at the book.
6. Don't keep at it too long at a stretch. Do a ten-minute spurt, go to something else, and come back later.
7. Concentrate on trouble spots and on transitions from one section to another. Make use of MNEMONIC DEVICES if they will help.
8. Recite the passage several times just before you go to sleep. You may wake up to find yourself word-perfect without conscious effort.
9. Once you've memorized the passage, say it over once a day to fix it in your mind.
10. If you're memorizing a part in a PLAY, be sure to learn the *cues*—the words or actions that come just before you speak or act.

metaphors see FIGURATIVE LANGUAGE, B.

meter see POETRY.

misplaced modifiers

A misplaced modifier is a word or group of words that is placed carelessly in a sentence so that it does not modify—relate to—the words that the writer intended it to.

Examples:

1. Misplaced.   George longed for cold weather
   in Death Valley.

   Corrected.   *In Death Valley* George longed
   for cold weather.

2. Misplaced.   She told us about falling off the
   cliff *in the corridor before class.*

   Corrected.   *In the corridor before class* she
   told us about falling off the cliff.

3. Misplaced.   *At age four* my father said that I
   could already dismantle a TV
   set.

   Corrected.   My father said that *at age four* I
   could already dismantle a TV
   set.

NOTE: Writers misplace modifiers because they
write as if they were speaking, forgetting that
in speech they use gestures and changes of
speed, stress, and tone of voice to help put
across their meaning. But in writing, the
reader has only the words on the page—no
gestures, no stress. After you write, therefore,
reread what you have written, trying to put
yourself in the position of the reader, *outside*
the writing, who gets his idea of what you are
saying only from the written words. Are there
ways that your words can lead the reader's
mind astray? Try to read your writing as if
you were a stranger to it. See REVISION OF
PAPERS and PROOFREADING. See also MODIFIERS.

mixed metaphors   see FIGURATIVE LANGUAGE, B.

mnemonic devices

A mnemonic device is a trick to enable you to
remember something, such as the proper spelling of a
certain word. The SPELLING RULES are, in a sense,
mnemonic devices. There are a few other devices for
helping you to remember the spelling of certain difficult
words. The SPELLING DEMONS list contains yet others.

cemetery (Scream "eee!" in the cemetery.)
exis*ten*ce (A cat has *ten* existences.)

h*ear* (hear with your *ear*)
lon*eli*ness (*Eli* in his loneliness)
pecu*liar* (a peculiar *liar*)
*secret*ary (A secretary keeps a *secret*.)
station*ery* (is pap*er*)
*villa*in (the villain in his *villa*)

You can probably make some devices on your own
—it doesn't matter how crazy they are—that will help
you remember how to spell many of the words that
cause you most trouble.

modifiers

Modifiers are words that change the meaning of
other words by describing or limiting them. The most
common modifiers are ADJECTIVES and ADVERBS, which
usually modify NOUNS and VERBS respectively. The
noun *crime*, for example, standing alone, is quite a
broad idea in our minds. But with modifiers—

the crime;

one petty crime;

George's strange, habitual crime
—it becomes more precise and limited. The verb
vibrate, to take another example, can be modified by
various adverbs:

vibrate *loudly*;

never vibrate;

vibrate *intermittently*.
The modifiers affect the meaning of *vibrate*. Nouns
and verbs can also be modified by PHRASES, CLAUSES,
and other nouns: *"kitchen* sink."
(noun)

The subject of modification is complicated and
often subtle. One can say, in fact, that every word in

a sentence modifies every other word, since without any one of its parts the sentence, and all the words in it, would change. As you write, it is important, and sometimes difficult, to make your patterns of modification clear to the reader. Usually it is a matter of using your ear for language and your good sense, but sometimes you need to do some exact thinking.

See MISPLACED MODIFIERS.

_____

_____

_____

_____

_____

_____

_____

_____

_____

_____

_____

M

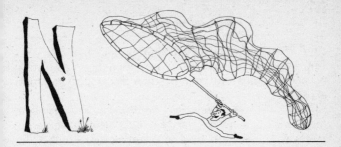

note-taking

Skill in taking notes is useful in several situations.

A. *Gathering information for and organizing reports*

For most REPORTS you must collect information from a number of sources, more than you could remember without notes. It is handy to write notes on 3 x 5 cards so that you can arrange and rearrange them afterward to fit the ORGANIZATION of your paper. Be sure to record your sources: title, author, date, and so on; see FOOTNOTES and BIBLIOGRAPHY.

B. *Reading for a course*

If you do not own the book you are reading to satisfy the needs of a particular course, you will need to take notes so that you can review the information later to reinforce your learning and to prepare for a test. Notes on reading can be taken on notebook paper or on yellow pads.

C. *Learning from a speaker*

When you want or are assigned to remember the ideas of a speaker whose lecture you are attending, notes will help. With practice you can learn to detect the organization of the speaker's remarks; you will be alert to such phrases as "first," or "another main idea is," or any other ways of pointing to a generalization, a supporting point or fact, or a·conclusion. Because you may need to write key points and words rather quickly, it will be especially helpful to review and, if necessary, expand notes soon afterward in order to fill in from memory any points that may not be clear.

N

D. *Learning from an interview*

Be sure that you record accurately the name of, position of, and other important information about the person you are interviewing. Your situation as an interviewer is similar to your position as the listener to a speaker. But you must also think of your next question even as you listen and make your notes. Further, you may ask the person interviewed to slow down for a moment to give you time to record a major point. In interviewing, your job will be easier if you prepare your questions in advance—even though you should be ready to change or abandon them if a new idea comes up or if the question is answered before you ask it.

E. *Learning from class lectures and discussions*

Many people find it helpful to keep a notebook open and pencil poised during presentations by a teacher or during discussion. In this way important facts, conclusions, recommended reading, suggestions for review, and any other important matters can be recorded for later review and study.

GUIDES FOR TAKING AND USING NOTES

1. Note your sources accurately (see the first paragraph of this section).
2. Use your own words to express the ideas you read or hear.
3. If you quote the words of the source exactly, use quotation marks, and note the page of the book or other publication from which the quotation is taken. Using the words of others without quotation marks and credit to the source is called PLAGIARISM.
4. Abbreviate and condense to save time and space, but not so drastically that you cannot recall later what your notes mean. Many people develop short-hand symbols and abbreviations for commonly used words. For example, "w/o" = without; "∴" = therefore; "c" = approximately. For a report on the Industrial Revolution or on Martin Luther King, your

notes need only record "IR" or "MLK" (or even "K").

5. Note only key words and figures to jog your memory, but be sure you write enough so that the notes will not become meaningless to you later.

Example:

Passage: *"Physical addiction* is a craving for a drug, a need for it so overpowering that it becomes the addict's most important concern. He feels he cannot live without the drug and his life becomes committed to the quest for it."

Inadequate note: phys. a. craving imp. concern

Adequate note: phys. addict'n: craving, overpowering need; addict feels must have drug to live, so becomes top concern.

6. Look over your notes at your earliest convenience to be sure they are clear to you and to clarify them if they are not. You may underline and excerpt from your notes right in the margin of the page or card, perhaps in ink of another color. This device will help fix the material in your mind.

See also REPORTS; REVIEWING FOR TESTS AND EXAMS.

nouns

A noun is a word used to name a person, place, or thing. It is one of the PARTS OF SPEECH.

Examples:

1. boy, cosmonaut, grammarian, Lincoln [persons]
2. Bermuda, home, school, world [places]
3. perspiration, rod, sandals [things]

Nouns are used in sentences mainly as SIMPLE SUBJECT, OBJECT, and COMPLEMENT.

Examples:

1. My *dog* sank his *teeth* into your *arm*.
   (simp. subj.)   (obj.)   (obj. of prep.)

N

2. Over the   *fence*   jumped three *kangaroos*
           (obj. of prep.)   (simp. subj.)
followed by a *helicopter*.
      (obj. of prep.)

3. My favorite   *comedian*   is an   *addict*   and
              (simp. subj.)   (compl.)
poet.
(compl.)

NOTES:
1. Any word that becomes plural (more than one) by adding *s* or *es* is a noun: "one crutch, two crutches."
2. Any word that becomes possessive by adding *'s* or just *'* (apostrophe) is a noun: "the *ship's* propeller," "the *housemaid's* knee," "those *creeps'* blue jeans."
3. PROPER NOUNS are special names and are capitalized: "Denver," "Denise."

A FRAME TEST for nouns is: "I am happy about (the) _____."
                                       (noun)

novels

A novel is a piece of prose fiction of considerable length, much longer than a SHORT STORY. It commonly contains characters whose actions and thoughts are quite fully developed according to some pattern or plot.

numbers

In formal writing all numbers below one hundred and all round numbers (a thousand, a million) should be written out, except in dates, addresses, and tables or sets of statistics and the like, which contain many numbers making it awkward to write out even the short ones. Numbers above a hundred, unless they are short, should be written in figures.

Example:

In my thirty-three years of collecting, I have preserved 1035 different butterflies belonging to 106 species. My sixteen aunts and uncles and my

137 first and second cousins (or is it 138?) haven't done nearly as well.

NOTE: Use a hyphen between the words of a number below a hundred: "forty-five," "ninety-seven."

_____

_____

_____

_____

_____

_____

_____

_____

_____

_____

_____

_____

_____

_____

_____

_____

object

The object in a SENTENCE is most commonly the word or words that receive the action of the VERB. Used thus, it is called the DIRECT OBJECT, or the object of the verb.

Examples:

1. Moses *hammered* his   *idea*   home.
         (verb)   (direct obj.)

2. His present *pleased* the   *queen.*
          (verb)   (direct obj.)

Two other kinds of grammatical objects are IN-DIRECT OBJECT and *object of preposition*. The object of a preposition is the noun or pronoun that follows a preposition and is the last word in a prepositional phrase (see PHRASES).

Examples:

1. He put his foot   in his   *mouth.*
                   (obj. of prep.)
            (prepositional phrase)

2. Over the   *fence*   flew a loudly quacking
            (obj. of prep.)
     (prepositional phrase)
duck.

objective form or case   see CASES; PRONOUNS.

objects of preposition   see PHRASES, A.

organization

Organization is an important skill in writing and speaking. The challenge is to arrange your ideas or topics in a way that makes sense and conveys the

intended meaning. There is no set of easy tricks that
will enable you to organize the elements of a complicated subject, and in most cases there is probably no
single best plan of organization; several can work
equally well. And of course you must be able to *think*
in an organized way before you can write and speak
organized words. However, OUTLINING is a device that
will help you keep your thinking straight. So will
holding in mind the pattern of *beginning, middle,* and
end (see ESSAYS, C). NOTE-TAKING on 3 x 5 cards is
also an aid to organizing a long paper, since the cards
can easily be arranged and rearranged.

outlining

An outline is a systematic statement of the order,
structure, and content of REPORTS, ESSAYS, SHORT
STORIES, SPEECHES, or other organized compositions. It
is usually arranged in main topics and subtopics and
provides a working plan for the projected work or
speech.

An outline is a tool to help organize thoughts. An
informal or rough outline consists of a simple listing
of the main ideas of the speech or composition you are
working on, with enough space between each item to
allow examples, facts, incidents, and other supporting
material to be inserted under each of the main ideas.

A more formal outline, following a prescribed pattern, is carefully worked out to show the ideas for a
piece in relation to each other. An example of such an
outline is on page 92.

Except when it is assigned as an exercise in form,
an outline should be the servant of the writer or
speaker, not the dominator. An outline should be
subject to revision and reordering both as it is first
made and also as the writing proceeds. Often the actual
writing will show that the outline needs revision. In
general the PARAGRAPHS of a composition tend to follow
the main elements of the outline.

O

A Form for Outlining

I. Introduction

  A. First point
     1. Subpoint
     2. Subpoint

  B. Second point
     1.
       a.
       b.
     2.

[Never introduce a subtopic unless you can give at least two instances (A, B; 1, 2).]

II. First main section of topic

  A. Subtopic
     1.
       a.
       b.
     2.
     3.
       a.
       b.
         (1)
         (2)

[Points and subpoints to establish and develop Subtopic A.]

  B. Subtopic
     1.
     2.
       a.
       b.
         (1)
         (2)
       c.

NOTES:
1. Roman numerals are used for the main topics.
2. Subtopics are marked with capital letters, then Arabic numerals, then small letters, and so on.
3. Each lower rank of topic is further indented.
4. The topics and subtopics are usually expressed as NOUNS, noun phrases, or questions; the first word of each is capitalized.

O

paragraphs

Paragraphs (except in DIALOGUE) are a series of sentences that develop one topic or a section of a longer topic. The paragraph is almost always a division of a longer piece of writing; it seldom stands alone, except in school assignments. Each paragraph generally contains a main idea or point, commonly supported by additional material—facts, opinions, examples, and the like. If there is one sentence that states the topic of the paragraph, it is called the *topic sentence*, and often it comes at the beginning. When writing, indicate a paragraph clearly by indenting about an inch; when typing, indent five or ten spaces. (For further suggestions on paragraphing as a part of a longer paper see ESSAYS, D.)

It can be good practice to develop a coherent single paragraph. The traditional way is to state the topic or main idea of the paragraph in a *topic sentence*. Next, *develop* the topic by sentences relating to it. Such sentences usually present facts, examples, or incidents to support the topic. The paragraph you are reading is an example of how to develop a topic.

In a good piece of writing the ideas flow smoothly from one paragraph to the next. For suggestions on how to achieve this flow, see TRANSITIONS.

For another use of paragraphs, see DIALOGUE, 10.

parallel construction

Parallel construction applies to the practice of writing sentences in such a way that a series of grammatical elements are of the same type rather than awkwardly and unintentionally varied.

Examples:

Parallel	*Nonparallel* (bad writing)
1. I came, I saw, I conquered.	1. I came and then, when I saw, I was able to conquer.
2. He favored government of the people, by the people, for the people.	2. He favored government of the people, thought it should be by the people, and done for them.
3. Let a man overcome anger by love, evil by good, the greedy by liberality, the liar by truth. —BUDDHA	3. Let a man overcome anger by love, make evil lose to good, defeat greed by liberality, and put down a liar by telling the truth.
4. My arguments are simple: it is ugly, it is smelly, and my mother is against it.	4. My arguments are simple: it is ugly, and the smell is terrible. Also opposed to it is my mother.
5. Because she never had been to Dallas before, because she was timid and hungry, and because she loved a man in Chicago, Jessica decided to take the next flight out.	5. Because she had never been to Dallas before, and also she was timid and hungry, and, in addition, she loved a man in Chicago, Jessica decided to take the next flight out.

NOTE: In catching awkward, nonparallel passages in your own writing, your ear will probably be of even more help to you than your knowledge of grammar. Read your writing aloud to catch nonparallelisms; then correct them.

P

parentheses

Parentheses are used to enclose words that are outside the main thought of the sentence or paragraph or are in some way extraneous.

Examples:

1. Please order twenty-five (25) copies of the book.
2. I had never really understood what he said (perhaps he intended it that way), and therefore he remained a stranger to me.
3. My mother (at least I was later told she was my mother) left me when I was still in diapers.

NOTES:

1. Do not overuse parentheses. Commas are usually more effective. Especially do not use parentheses to insert some information (such as the name of a character in a story) that should have been established at the beginning. Instead of the parentheses, revise the paper so that the omitted idea appears in its proper place. Parentheses can become the crutch of a lazy writer.
2. In *The Practical Stylist* Sheridan Baker writes, "The DASH says aloud what the parenthesis whispers. Both enclose interruptions too extravagant for a pair of commas to hold."*

participial phrases   see PHRASES, B; PARTICIPLES.

participles

Participles are verbs in the -ing or -ed form when they are used to modify NOUNS or PRONOUNS (see also MODIFIERS).

---

*Sheridan Baker, *The Practical Stylist*, 3rd ed., New York (Thomas Y. Crowell Company), 1973, p. 72.

Examples:

verb	participle	noun modified
burn	burning	houses
edit	edited	books
run	running	water
scramble	scrambled	eggs

Very often participles are used in *phrases*, forming participal phrases.

Examples:

1. *Entering the room,* I tripped over the cat.
   (part. phrase)   (pronoun)

2. The English *textbook* disappeared out the
   (noun)

   window, *hurled by an irate student.*
   (part. phrase)

NOTES:

1. Experienced writers use participial phrases (and many other grammatical elements) almost effortlessly as their "ear" for the words and rhythm of language tells them how to control the flow of their sentences. Inexperienced writers may need to be quite deliberate as they experiment in using such phrases, especially to break up the monotony of many short, simple sentences, uninterrupted, one after another.

Examples:

1. Simple sentences:
   The puppy chased after his own tail. He wore a hole in the rug.
   Sentence with participial phrase:
   Chasing after his own tail, the puppy wore a hole in the rug.

2. Simple:
   The next thing I knew, there was Dad. He was trembling with rage.
   Sentence with participial phrase:
   The next thing I knew, there was Dad, *trembling with rage.*

The second sentence of the second example is not necessarily better than the first; it depends on the context in which the sentences appear and the emphasis you want to achieve. See also DANGLING PARTICIPIAL PHRASES.

2. Be careful not to punctuate a participial phrase as if it were a sentence.
Example:
Wrong: The next thing I knew, there was Dad. Trembling with rage.
See SENTENCE FRAGMENTS.

parts of speech

Parts of speech are the classes of words in a language. In traditional grammar the words of English are divided into eight parts of speech: NOUNS, PRONOUNS, VERBS, ADJECTIVES, ADVERBS, PREPOSITIONS, CONJUNCTIONS, and INTERJECTIONS. In reality no language can be divided neatly into eight "parts," and it is often not possible to determine the part of speech to which a word belongs until you know how it is used in a sentence.

Examples:
1. The *cook* spoiled the broth. [noun]
2. She will *cook* your goose. [verb]

If you need to know the parts of speech a particular word can be, consult a DICTIONARY.

The following is a convenient summary of the parts of speech. More details about each are given under its alphabetical entry.

part of speech	how used	examples
noun	as name of person, place or thing	ostrich, Mabel, destination
pronoun	to take the place of or refer to a noun	it, she, everybody
verb	to help express action or make a statement	gallop, speak, were
adjective	to modify a noun or pronoun	ugly, glamorous, putrid
adverb	to modify a verb (or adjective or another adverb)	gladly, very, yesterday
preposition	to begin a prepositional phrase	*to* the end; *over* the hill

part of speech	how used	examples
conjunction	to join words or other elements	and, but, or, because, although
interjection	to show feeling with a single word	whoopee! ugh! wow!

NOTE: Modern grammars distinguish between two kinds of parts of speech:

1. *Unlimited word classes* are NOUNS, VERBS, ADJECTIVES, and ADVERBS (and, less important, INTERJECTIONS). The language contains an indefinite—unlimited—number of these words, since new ones frequently enter the language and old ones sometimes die out.

2. *Structure words* are DETERMINERS, PRONOUNS, PREPOSITIONS, and CONJUNCTIONS (as well as *linking* and *auxiliary verbs*). Structure words, which are strictly limited in number, give shape—structure—to English sentences. In the following sentence the structure words are italicized and labeled:

    "*Three* hens suddenly attacked *six*
    (determiner)   (determiner)
    roosters *in* *the* barnyard
          (preposition) (determiner)
    because *they* disliked
    (subordinating conjunction) (pronoun)
    the farmer's sexist prejudices."
    (determiner)

    Note that when the nouns, verbs, adjectives, and adverbs in the sentence above are changed to nonsense words but the structure words remain, the sentence still sounds like a sentence; that is, it has shape or structure. "*Three* gombashes mumply clorbed *six* scrimbles *in the* kasterpitz *because* *they* froppolated *the* pamfarce's oggish prunks."

passive voice   see VOICE.

patterns of sentences   see SENTENCE PATTERNS.

P

periods (.)

The period is a punctuation mark that is used as follows:

> 1. Use a period at the end of any sentence that is not a question or an exclamation.

Example:

My sister married a professor.

2. Use a period after abbreviations.

Examples:

N.J. (New Jersey); gals. (gallons); Mr. (mister).

Some abbreviations customarily omit periods.

Examples:

NASA (National Aeronautics and Space Administration); WAC (Women's Army Corps); UFO (Unidentified Flying Object).

When in doubt, refer to a dictionary. Words of abbreviation formed from the initials of a proper name are called *acronyms*.

personification   see FIGURATIVE LANGUAGE.

persuasion

To persuade or convince people is a principal PURPOSE of writing and speaking. To be able to persuade others that a fact is true, that an idea is sound, that certain actions should be undertaken or avoided, that a given program is good or bad is a valuable skill. Three important ways that people use to persuade others are conversation, SPEECH MAKING, and writing. (They also persuade by the example of their actions.)

In the long run you make the most persuasive argument when you have a good case, when you yourself are thoroughly convinced of it, and when you present your arguments with sincerity and in a well-organized manner. There are some devices—or even tricks—you can use. They can help your cause, but they won't (or shouldn't, anyway) make a bad case good. (See also DEBATING.)

A. *Analyzing*

The first step in developing a persuasive case is to *analyze the subject*. You should know all the arguments for and against your point of view. You may find it helpful to list the arguments in two columns. Be sure that the arguments you use are relevant or pertinent to your case, that they do not wander off onto other subjects.

B. *Gathering material*

You will probably need to gather information and ideas through reading and talking with people. Don't ignore facts and ideas that go against your case, since the people you are trying to persuade may well know of them; if you are unaware of the opposing material, you weaken your argument. Take notes (see NOTE-TAKING).

C. *Organizing*

When you have gathered your material, or as you gather it, you will need to organize it. See ESSAYS, OUTLINING, and ORGANIZATION. Some methods that can be useful in persuading others are listed below.

1. *Citing facts* to support your view, naming their sources if the facts are likely to be doubted.

2. *Relating relevant incidents or experiences* in which you or others have been involved. A vividly told experience is memorable and convincing, perhaps more so than it should be.

3. *Citing authorities* who support your view—a famous doctor on a medical question, a respected teacher or principal on an educational question, and the like. Brief direct quotations from the authority are impressive. (See also QUOTATION MARKS.)

4. *Using humor* and *funny stories* to hold the interest of your readers or listeners. Be sure, however, that you don't drag in a joke simply to get a laugh. The funny story should illustrate your argument in a memorable way.

5. *Using association* to establish a link between things everyone likes (nice people, good feelings, love, sunny and warm places, adventure, and so on) and the point of view for which you are arguing; or associating the opposing point of view with things people don't like (murder, hate, cold, dark places, and so forth). Be careful, however, when you use association, since the device can be merely a cheap propaganda trick, somewhat dishonest, and is likely to backfire.

6. *Making a direct appeal,* once you have established your case, by expressing your conviction with sincerity and feeling.

7. *Appealing to emotions,* if the subject is one you feel deeply about. Sharing your emotion with the audience in an effort to arouse your listeners' or readers' feelings can strengthen the impact of your case. Don't, however, let the emotion drown the thinking.

phrases

A phrase is a group of words related in some way (often acting in a sentence as a single PART OF SPEECH) and not containing a SUBJECT and VERB. CLAUSES and SENTENCES do contain subjects and verbs; phrases generally do not. There are four main types of phrases in English.

A. *The prepositional phrase* starts with a PREPOSITION and ends with its object.

> *Example:*
> The rock band fell *through*   the *floor*.
>   (prep.)   (obj. of prep.)

A prepositional phrase may be used as an ADJECTIVE (modifying a NOUN) or as an ADVERB (modifying a VERB).

Examples:

1. adjective phrase: The *boys   on the roof*
                       (noun) (adj. phrase)
   shouted obscenities.

2. adverb phrase: Tom *ate on the roof.*
                      (verb) (adv. phrase)

B. *The participial phrase* starts with a participle and contains words that relate to it.

Examples:

Seeing his baby brother, George hid the balloon.

There was Mary, *flirting with the seniors again.*

As you can see, participial phrases modify nouns and thus are adjective phrases. (See also DANGLING PARTICIPIAL PHRASES.)

C. *The appositive phrase* is a group of words that follow a noun and give information about the noun. (See also APPOSITIVES.)

Example:

Politics, *a noble profession,* is the art of the
(noun)   (appos. phrase)
possible.

D. *The verb phrase* is a main verb and the auxiliaries (or helping verbs) that go with it.

Example:

They *had   been   weeping*   silently until
       (aux.)   (aux.)   (main vb.)
someone gave them ten dollars.

> NOTE: Another type is the *transitional phrase* (see TRANSITIONS), which helps carry the mind of the reader or listener from one section of a paper or speech to the next.
> *Examples:*
> on the other hand, in a similar way, at the same time.

See also GERUND PHRASES; INFINITIVE PHRASES.

P

plagiarism

Plagiarism is the act of appropriating and passing off as one's own the words or ideas of another person. Copying another person's paper, taking the ideas from a TV program and using them without giving credit to the source, and lifting passages from an article or encyclopedia for use in a report are examples of plagiarism.

In NOTE-TAKING and in reading for REPORTS, be sure to make an exact record of where your ideas come from. If you quote directly from a work, use quotation marks and identify your source in the text of the paper or in a footnote (see FOOTNOTES). When you express an idea that is not common knowledge, an idea that you found in your reading, you should inform your reader of the source even if you express the information in your own words (paraphrase it).

Plagiarism is quite common in schools, especially in the writing of reports. It is likely that much of it results from ignorance of the proper procedures rather than from the intent to be dishonest.

plays

A play, or drama, is a literary form in which the words and actions of actors on a stage convey a true or invented story to an audience. It takes special skill to write DIALOGUE for a play in a way that will seem real or will achieve the effect you desire. It is fun, and a good chance to practice various skills, to write short skits or dramatic scenes to be acted in class or at another gathering.

When writing a play or a scene, you may find it helpful to follow a standard form. Obviously, in a real play no scene would be as brief, and probably not as inconsequential, as the following one.

The Cart Before the Horse

Cast of Characters
CULLY MILLER, an ice-cream parlor operator
JEZEBEL, his daughter
FRANKLIN, a neighborhood horse
MAYELLA, driver of the cart

Place and time: A small town in upper New York state, about 1890, midsummer.

SCENE I

On the sidewalk just outside Cully's Ice-Cream Parlor. It is late afternoon. Three small tables, each with two chairs, are placed in front of store window. At rise: CULLY MILLER, about 55, weary and perspiring, stands down center, looking discouraged.

CULLY (*after a moment of silent slouching and a deep sigh*). I might as well give up. Without ice, how can I make ice cream. Without ice cream—

JEZEBEL (*running in from left and shouting*). Father! Father! I have found a supply of ice.

CULLY. Go away.

(*They look at each other silently for a moment,* CULLY *in weary discouragement,* JEZEBEL *excited but let down by her father's response.*)

JEZEBEL (*slowly crossing and sitting in chair, right*). But, Father, listen. Mayella and Franklin are coming. They're only half a block away.

CURTAIN

In most school situations, any plays or scenes you write will probably be performed informally—without stage, curtain, or scenery. A few *properties* (props) and a suggestion or two of *costume* will be all that is needed. If the acting is good, the imagination of the audience can perform wonders. Instead of scenery you may use a *narrator*, who will tell the audience what scene they are to imagine. The narrator can also tell the audience whatever they need to know as the play proceeds from scene to scene or from one period of time to another. (A famous example of the use of a narrator is in Thornton Wilder's play *Our Town*.)

In writing *stage directions*, you will need to tell the actors and scenery designers where to move or to place objects. Directions (left, right, center) are always given from the point of view of the actors, not the audience. *Upstage* means away from the audience, *downstage* means toward the audience.

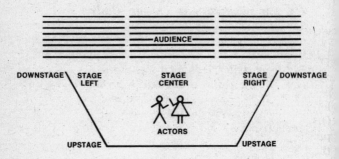

plural

Plural means more than one, as distinguished from *singular*, one only. Most nouns in English form their plural by adding *s* (boy, boys); words ending in *s*, *sh*, *ch*, and *x* add *es* [box, box*es*; church, church*es*]. Most, but not all, nouns ending in *o* add *es* for the plural [hero, hero*es*; potato, potato*es*]. Some words form their plurals in irregular ways [child, children; louse, lice]. To find the correct plural of a word, consult a dictionary. Words ending in *y* present special problems; most commonly the *y* changes to *ies* [baby, babies]; see also SPELLING RULE, 4.

poetry

Poetry is a kind of writing, generally rhythmic,

designed to convey to the reader or hearer a vivid, imaginative sense of experience. Some characteristics of poetry are

> use of condensed language
> use of words chosen for their sound and power of suggestion
> use of FIGURATIVE LANGUAGE
> use of rhyme
> use of meter (measured rhythm or beat)

One great poet, Robert Frost, explained, "Poetry is a *made* thing."

The opposite of poetry is *prose*, which is simply "not poetry." Some prose is quite poetic, some poetry is quite prosaic—there's no clear line between them. Poetry tends to deal with feelings and emotion.

Conventional poetry is written in groups of lines called *stanzas*. Each poetic line begins with a capital letter even though the line does not begin a sentence. Other than that, poetry is punctuated exactly like prose. Much conventional poetry is rhymed; that is, the lines end in words whose last syllables or syllable sound the same, except for the opening letter. It is also *metric*; that is, the lines have a more or less regular beat. The following poem illustrates all these characteristics.

Dust of Snow	
The way a crow	1
Shook down on me	2
The dust of snow	3
From a hemlock tree	4
Has given my heart	5
A change of mood	6
And saved some part	7
Of a day I had rued.	8

[regretted or felt sorrowful about]

—ROBERT FROST

P

The poem is written in *iambic* meter—that is, in *feet* in each of which the first syllable is *unstressed* and the second one *stressed*: ta-DUM, ta-DUM (The wáy ă crŏw). Each line contains two iambic feet, except for lines 4 and 8, which are deliberately irregular. The poem is perfectly rhymed: A B A B C D C D is the *rhyme scheme*, in which the sound *ow* is A, *ee* is B, and so on (crow A, me B, snow A, tree B).

Iambic meter is the most often used in poetry because the English language falls rather naturally into that pattern: Now as you read this book you'll see that it is best to concentrate on topics that you need to learn and leave the rest alone. The second most common meter is *trochaic*, in which the feet go: DUM-ta, DUM-ta:

> Then the little Hiawatha
> Learned of every bird its language

When poetry is rhymed and metered, it is called *bound verse*; when it has meter but no rhyme, it is called *blank verse*; when it is neither rhymed nor metered, it is *free verse*. It requires time and craftsmanship to write good bound or blank verse. Bad bound verse is about as bad as anything can be—the rhymes are forced, and the meter gets in the way of the ideas and feeling. Don't think that just because you've written a couple of lines that rhyme, you've made a poem. For example,

> You have in front of you this lovely book,
> And all you have to do is look and look.

is not poetry; it's merely two metered lines that rhyme. It has none of the other characteristics of poetry. Inexperienced writers are likely to do better with free verse, which leaves them more freedom to concentrate on ideas, feelings, metaphor, and vigor.

When you read poetry aloud, it should be read
slowly (it's condensed and cannot be absorbed rapidly
like prose); you should not stress the rhyme and
meter but read for the meaning and let the rhyme and
meter take care of themselves; and you should hold
your voice up at the end of the lines unless the punctuation or sense shows that a sentence has ended. For
example, the entire poem "Dust of Snow" is a single
sentence, and it should be read accordingly, perhaps
with the very slightest stress on the rhymed words
but no full stop after any line because the sense does
not come to an ending until the word "rued."

possessive   see APOSTROPHES.

possessive case   see CASES; PRONOUNS.

predicates   see SENTENCES, A.

prefixes

A prefix is a syllable or syllables added to the
beginning of a word to change its meaning. Prefixes are
one of the elements that make up many words, others
being suffixes and roots. Most prefixes in English have
their origin in Greek or Latin. It will help you to figure
out the meaning of many words to know what some of
the common prefixes mean. All prefixes are listed in
the dictionary.

Latin prefixes

prefix	meaning	examples in word
ab-	away	abduct, abnormal
ad-	toward, to	adjourn, administer
anti-	against	antiaircraft, anti-feminist
bi-	two	biped, binomial
co-	with	cooperate, coauthor
com-, con-	with	concur, combine
dis-	reverse of	disobey, disadvantage

P

prefix	meaning	examples in word
ex-	out of	excavate, exclude
extra-	beyond, outside	extraordinary, extra-sensory
in-	into, not	include, incapable
inter-	together, between	intertwine, international
intra-	within	intramural, intra-cardiac
mis-	bad, wrong	misadventure, mistake
non-	not	nonaligned, nonsense
post-	after	postgraduate, post-operative
pre-, pro-	before, forth	prepare, project
re-	back, again	regress, reread
semi-	half	semiconscious, semi-skilled
sub-	under	subconscious, sub-cutaneous
super-	above, greater	superstructure, super-tanker
trans-	across	transportation, trans-atlantic

Greek prefixes

prefix	meaning	examples in word
auto-	self	autohypnosis, auto-biography
hydro-	water	hydroelectric, hydro-phobia
micro-	small	microscope, micro-biology
ortho-	right, straight	orthodox, orthodontia
sym-	together	symphony, symbiotic
tri-	three	triangle, trisect

NOTES:
1. In general, a prefix changes the meaning of a word or root, whereas a SUFFIX usually

changes its function (PART OF SPEECH) or TENSE.

2. When you add a prefix to a root, you do not change its spelling or that of the root: *mis + spell = misspell*; *dis + appear = disappear*. However, over the history of our language, the spelling of a good many prefixes has changed through the effect of *assimilation*. Thus, "in-migrant" has become *immigrant*, while an "out-migrant" is an *emigrant* (from *ex + migrant*).

prepositional phrases   see PHRASES.

prepositions

A preposition is a word that shows the relationship of a NOUN or PRONOUN to some other word in a SENTENCE. Prepositions are commonly used in a PREPOSITIONAL PHRASE. There are about fifty prepositions in English. Among the most common are:

about	between	off
above	beyond	on
according to	by	over
across	down	through
after	during	to
around	for	toward
at	from	under
before	in	until
behind	instead of	up
below	into	with
beside	of	without

A FRAME TEST that works pretty well for prepositions, except *of*, is:

"It went _____ the thing(s)."
                    (preposition)

See also PARTS OF SPEECH.

principal parts

Principal parts are the four basic forms of a VERB:

P

the present, the past, the present PARTICIPLE, and the past participle. In regular verbs, these are as follows.

present	past	present participle	past participle
look	looked	looking	(have) looked
experience	experienced	experiencing	(have) experienced

Irregular verbs form the parts differently:

present	past	present participle	past participle
eat	ate	eating	(have) eaten
go	went	going	(have) gone

The principal parts of irregular verbs are listed in DICTIONARIES, usually immediately following the entry word and preceding the definitions.

See also TENSES.

pronoun references   see PRONOUNS.

pronouns

A pronoun is a word used in place of a NOUN (see PARTS OF SPEECH). The pronoun almost always refers to the noun that immediately precedes it (goes before it) and is so understood by the reader or listener. In the following sentences the arrows point from the pronouns back to the nouns they refer to (called *antecedents*).

Examples:

1. Black is the color of my true love's hair. She

   dyes it.

2. A glimpse of the criminal was all I got, but

   it was enough to identify her.

3. Grandma clung to the pillar so hard it col-

lapsed on her.

One problem in writing is the difficulty of making the antecedent of a pronoun absolutely clear, thus obscuring the meaning of the sentence.

Examples:

1. Lennie and Red went into *his* house. [Problem: whose house?]
2. Mr. Trimble told Mike *he* needed a vacation. [Problem: who needed?]

Many pronouns change form as they change CASE and *number*. The following chart lists the most common personal pronouns in English.

Subject Form		*Object Form*		*Possessive Form*	
Singular	*Plural*	*Singular*	*Plural*	*Singular*	*Plural*
I	we	me	us	my	our
you	you	you	you	your	your
he	they	him	them	his	their, theirs
she	they	her	them	her, hers	their, theirs

Other common pronouns are:

> this
> THAT
> these
> those
> each
> both
> some
> few
> much
> nobody
> none
> myself
> himself

herself
yourself
themselves
WHO
whose
whom

Another aspect is the necessity of making sure that pronouns *agree with their antecedents in number* (singular or plural).

Example:

Wrong.   *One* of the students lost   *their*   sneakers.
(pronoun)

Right.   *One* of the students lost   *his*   sneakers.
(pronoun)

NOTE: The possessive form of pronouns does not use an *apostrophe* (*hers, theirs,* and so on) with the exception of *one* (*one's* own thing).

proofreading

When a book is set in type, it is first printed on long sheets called galleys or *galley proofs.* The galleys are read by proofreaders—sharp-eyed experts who examine every word and punctuation mark with merciless care to catch and correct every error before the book or magazine is printed and sold.

You should be the proofreader of your own papers. Before you hand in any important piece of written work, make yourself a stranger to it and then read it as carefully as if you were a proofreader preparing it for publication. Reading it aloud to yourself will make sure that you do not miss any words. Try to get your papers done early enough to allow time for proofreading.

See also REVISION OF PAPERS and SYMBOLS TO GUIDE REVISION OF PAPERS.

proper adjectives

Proper ADJECTIVES are adjectives made from PROPER NOUNS. They are always capitalized.

Examples:
American
a *Pacific* storm
Chinese cooking
an *Indian* reservation

proper nouns

Proper nouns name a special or particular person, place or thing. They are always capitalized.

Example:

When my friend *Jeff* was robbing a bank in *Chicago*, he was shot down by *Mrs. Jessie Bloom*, the fiercest cop in town. But unfortunately he was saved by his brother *Jack*, from *Midlands Bank*, who arrived on a *Honda* motorcycle, creating wild confusion before he fled to *Gary, Indiana*.

public speaking   see SPEECH-MAKING.

punctuation

The main purpose of punctuation (the word comes from the Latin noun *punctus*, meaning "point") is to aid readers better to understand the meaning of a piece of writing, the relationships of words and ideas in sentences, and the emphasis and tone intended by the writer. Early in the history of language, especially before dictionaries and grammar books existed, writers had great freedom to punctuate as they desired; but today English has become conventionalized to the extent that in most instances there is only one correct way to punctuate a given passage. There is still some room for individuality in punctuation, however, and some modern writers choose to punctuate according to their own rules and feelings, less bound by the conventions than are more traditional writers. Even for traditional writers and in writing for school and college, however, there is considerable room for judgment as to exactly what punctuation will help convey the precise meaning and feeling the writer intends.

See also CONVENTIONS OF ENGLISH.

P

purpose

If you are to successfully write an ESSAY, REPORT, or SHORT STORY or make a SPEECH, you must be clear about your purpose and the nature of your readers or audience. (See WRITING FOR WHOM?) Your purpose may be one or more of the following: to give information; to persuade (see PERSUASION); to make an impression, as in a job or college application or interview; to entertain; to move to action or to stop action; to calm and soothe. As you prepare your work, keep asking yourself: Will this help accomplish the purpose I have in mind?

P

qualifiers

Qualifiers, sometimes called *intensifiers,* are a special small group of ADVERBS that modify ADJECTIVES and other adverbs.

> *Examples:*
> 1. He did it *very* *well.*
>   (qual.) (adv.)
>
> 2. The *very* *bright* light hurt his eyes.
>   (qual.) (adj.)

Any word that can be replaced by *very* and still make some kind of sense is a qualifier. The most common qualifiers are:

> awfully
> extremely
> more
> most
> pretty (He was *pretty* dirty.)
> quite
> rather
> really (Sit up *really* straight.)
> somewhat
> too
> very

question mark (?)

A question mark at the end of a sentence indicates a question.

> *Examples:*
> 1. When will you leave the house?
> 2. "How are you?" asked Harry.

Q

NOTES:
1. Putting a question mark at the end of any sentence, even a statement, will turn it into a question.
   Example:
   Statement: That's a house.
   Question: That's a house?
2. Unless you are writing a comic strip, never use more than one question mark to indicate a question, and never use an exclamation mark and a question mark together.
   Example:
   Wrong. How can I possible recite when I'm drowning?!
   If you mean that sentence to be an exclamation, use an exclamation mark only.

quotation marks (" ")

For the main use of quotation marks, see DIALOGUE. Whenever you are using—quoting—the exact words of someone else, indicate this fact by enclosing them in quotation marks (see NOTE-TAKING). In addition:

1. Use quotation marks to indicate the titles of stories, chapters, or articles within books or magazines.

   Example:

   In the book *How to Live Through Junior High School*, there is a chapter entitled "The Sleeping Lion Awakes."

2. Use quotation marks around a word or phrase if you wish to show it is a word you yourself would not normally use—that you wish, somehow, to separate yourself from it.

   Example:

   Even the old folks were "spooning" down by the lake shore.

reader's guide to periodical literature
see REFERENCE BOOKS.

reading

Reading is a subject too complicated to be discussed fully in a handbook. If you read well, you are fortunate. If you have difficulty with reading—if you proceed at a much slower pace than most of your classmates; if you cannot understand or remember what you read—discuss the problem with an English teacher or a guidance counselor and ask for help in identifying your problem and in finding ways to start solving it. Take the initiative; don't merely hope that reading difficulties will go away in time.

One of the major mistakes that people make—even people who have no reading disabiilty—is to think that there is just one way to read. Given a reading assignment, they simply sit down and read it. This can be a very inefficient use of time and mind. There are at least five types of reading:

1. *Skimming*, for a general overview of the material or to find specific items of information.
2. *Rapid, relaxed reading*, to enjoy a story or an account of something you are interested in.
3. *Close, active reading for mastery*, used with textbooks, encyclopedias, and other materials from which you must learn the main facts and ideas. (See STUDY SKILLS, 4-10.)
4. *Word-for-word reading* (perhaps aloud), for directions or for problems in mathematics and the sciences.

122

5. POETRY *reading* (best aloud), for levels of meaning, metaphor, feeling, sound.

When you have an assignment, get your mind set for the kind of reading that you think applies.

reading for mastery   see STUDY SKILLS, 4-10.

reference books
Reference books can be a great help to you in school work or on a job. If you are assigned a large topic for study or a report, look it up first in a recent *encyclopedia,* in order to get a good idea of the dimensions and main areas of the topic. This basic information will supply a framework for deeper study. However, *don't* be limited by the encyclopedia; it should be a starter, not a limitation.

The Reader's Guide to Periodical Literature lists by subject and author all the articles that have appeared in over a hundred magazines. It is quite easy to use, and a new issue comes out twice a month, making recent material accessible. Examine the *Reader's Guide*; you'll see how useful it is.

Further, don't overlook *atlases, almanacs,* and *special dictionaries* (*Roget's* THESAURUS for synonyms; *biographical dictionaries* for short accounts of well-known lives; *Who's Who* and special regional and topical editions of *Who's Who,* such as *Who's Who in the East* or *Who's Who in Education,* for data on important people now living); and *books of quotations.* All reference works are usually kept in one section of the LIBRARY. Take an hour some day to familiarize yourself with them. They can teach you much and save you time.

relative pronouns   see THAT, WHICH.

reports
Writing reports is a common and important task. The ability to compile a good written or oral report is a valuable skill. A number of steps are involved.

R

1. *Choose a manageable topic.*
   a. It should interest you; at the very least, you should be able to develop an interest in it.
   b. It should not be so broad as to limit you to vast general statements, which require either no special knowledge or great wisdom. (*Too broad:* "Fish"; "Industry in the United States"; "Space Travel"; "Science Fiction." Manageable: "How Fish Are Quick-Frozen"; "The Indianapolis Telephone Industry"; "Sputnik, the First Artificial Satellite"; "H. G. Wells' *The Time Machine:* Science Fiction Almost a Century Ago.")
   c. Information on your subject should be readily available. If the topic you have selected is of interest to you and of manageable scope but you can find no sources bearing on it, change to another topic.
2. *Collect information.* See ESSAYS, B. See also REFERENCE BOOKS; LIBRARIES; NOTE-TAKING; FOOTNOTES.
3. *Organize your material.* See ESSAYS, C; OUTLINING.
4. *Write a first draft,* allowing space for changes —additions, deletions, reorganization, rewriting. See REVISION OF PAPERS.
5. *Reread and revise your report.* See REVISION OF PAPERS.
6. *Proofread your report.* See PROOFREADING.
7. *Make a BIBLIOGRAPHY for your report* if you have used a number of sources.

Although the most important quality of a report is what it says and how well it says it, you can enhance its attractiveness, interest and readability by finding or making illustrations that will enable the reader to understand more clearly what you have written. If you use illustrations, give each one a caption (a brief explanation, usually under the picture) and refer in the text to the number of the illustration. For example, write (in PARENTHESES) "see Figure 3," immediately following the sentence that applies to the illustration.

Sometimes using a different color of ink and changing the style and size of printing for the main headings make it easier and more pleasant to follow the argument of the report. Give thought to how the text is set up on the pages.

A well-designed cover sheet with the title, the date and your name may also add clarity.

However, *do not* fancy up your report simply for the sake of making it look pretty. Your main effort should go into substance rather than appearance.

For suggestions about the oral presentation of reports, see SPEECH MAKING.

restrictive and nonrestrictive clause

A restrictive CLAUSE is one that is necessary to the basic meaning of a sentence; a nonrestrictive clause, while it adds information, can be removed without disturbing the basic meaning of a sentence. Restrictive clauses are essential; nonrestrictive clauses are nonessential. Restrictive clauses are not set off by commas from the rest of the sentence; nonrestrictive clauses are.

Examples:

1. Restrictive clause: A poem *that has been memorized by millions* is "Trees."
2. Nonrestrictive clause: "Trees," *which is a very silly poem,* is hard to memorize.

In the first instance the clause modifies the noun *poem* and "restricts" the meaning of the noun. The clause is essential; the sentence would not make much sense without it. Therefore, no commas. In the second case, the clause modifies "Trees" but does not "restrict" or limit it—there *is* only one "Trees." The clause is nonessential; the sentence would make perfectly good sense without it. Set it off with commas therefore.

An easier and almost foolproof way to tell whether you need to set off a clause with commas is to read the sentence aloud. If your voice naturally pauses before the *which, who,* or *whose,* set the clause off with a comma on either side; if there's no pause, leave out the commas.

reviewing for tests and exams

Since people's styles of learning differ, no one system of studying for tests and exams will work equally well for everyone. However, the following suggestions may be helpful.

1. Assemble all your materials: texts, past tests, any notes you have taken, work sheets given out during the course, a pencil and paper to make notes as you review.

2. Look over all the pages of the texts and other materials you are responsible for mastering. *Do not simply reread all the materials.* Remember you are reviewing, not reading new material for mastery. (See STUDY SKILLS, 4-10.)

   a. Read each heading to see if you can recall the material that follows. If you cannot, read it (or skim, if that is enough to recall it to your mind).

   b. Read each underlined or italicized word, each numbered series or list, each item you have marked in any way. Be sure that you understand the significance of all these.

   c. Look at any exercises and study questions that may be included to be sure you can do or answer all of them. Be sure you understand the reason for each.

   d. Memorize any lists, formulas, or rules you were assigned to know.

3. If you have a large quantity of material to

review and master, make notes on a separate sheet of paper or on cards of the main points or items. Then review these notes to see if you recall the material on which they are based. If you recall little or nothing, reread the material.

4. Review carefully all tests you have had during the period under review, and be sure you can answer all the questions.

5. As you go through this procedure, if you find that you have any questions, *note them down* and ask them in class, if possible a few days before the test. If there are parts that seem more difficult for you than for others, ask the teacher for an appointment to go over problem areas with you.

6. It is a good device to try to put yourself in the position of the teacher and think out what kind of test or exam *you* would compile to test a student's knowledge of the material. It may even help to try to read the teacher's mind.

7. Just before the test, reread your notes one last time.

8. Sleep long and well the night before the test, so that your mind will be fresh.

See also TAKING TESTS AND EXAMS.

revision of papers

You probably do not do your best writing right off the bat. If things go well, you may set down passages of good writing, but usually there will also be clumsy sections, things that don't fit, poor TRANSITIONS, awkward sentences or sentences that come in monotonous succession (see SENTENCE VARIETY), words that aren't quite right, and—no matter how carefully you have planned ahead—sections that need to be shifted to clarify the pattern of ORGANIZATION and make the paper easier to read.

When you are working on an important paper, therefore, you should probably write a *first draft,* which will almost certainly need to be revised in major ways. If you have time, it often helps to set the first draft aside for a day or two before reading it for revision. The distance makes it easier for you to approach the paper with a clear, objective eye. After you have made the needed revisions, write (in ink) or type a fresh copy.

Be a sharp-eyed, sharp-eared, sharp-minded critic of your own paper before you hand it in. Be sure to PROOFREAD the final draft.

After you get your paper back from a teacher, you will probably need to revise it again, to "correct" it. In that sense an English assignment may be compared to football practice. If the team runs a play wrong, the coach will probably call the players back and say, "That's wrong. Here's how you should have run it." After he has explained, he will not say, "Okay, let's do the next play." Rather, he'll order, "Now run it right!" In this way the team learns to perform the plays correctly.

When you write a paper you will probably make some errors in SPELLING, PUNCTUATION, CAPITALIZATION, and SENTENCE structure, no matter how carefully you have proofread. The teacher may suggest some changes, perhaps in sequence and organization, development of ideas, strengthening of the argument, clearing up ambiguities, and eliminating needless repetition. Benefit from the corrections and suggestions; they are directed specifically at you. Revise your paper; make all the corrections; in other words, "Run it right!" Sometimes you learn more from revising a paper than you did from first writing it.

See also SYMBOLS TO GUIDE REVISION OF PAPERS; PROOFREADING.

rhyme   see POETRY.

roots of words

Roots are words or parts of words from which other words grow. In English many word roots come from

Greek and Latin. A common Greek root is *phone* or *phono*, which came from the Greek *phōnē* ("voice"). Such words as *telephone, phonetic, phonograph, megaphone*, and *microphone* are built on this root. You will be able to think of many English words that grow from the following roots.

root	meaning	sample words
bio	life	biography, biosphere
cide	killer, killing	suicide, pesticide
geo	earth	geology, geography
graph	write	autograph, telegraph
logy	science, study	biology, astrology
mega	great	megaphone, megalopolis
ped	foot	pedal, pedestrian
phobia	fear	claustrophobia, musophobia (mice)
script	write	manuscript, description
spec	look	spectator, inspect
thermo	heat	thermometer, thermostat

DICTIONARIES often include roots as a part of the history of a word, printing them in small caps:: "BIO-"; alternatively, they may be listed separately with a definition: "bio-." If you form the habit of looking at these roots when you're referring to a dictionary, it will help you enlarge your VOCABULARY.

run-on sentences

Run-on sentences are two sentences run together as if they were one. The best way to avoid this error is to *read your papers aloud* in a natural manner and listen for the place where your voice both pauses *and* drops in pitch. A pause and a drop in pitch almost certainly marks the end of a sentence (except for question sentences, which are a special case).

How to eliminate run-on sentences (r-o)

Here are two examples of incorrect run-on sentences:

Wrong: 1. Mabel flew down the stairs, she was in a hurry.

R

Wrong: 2. John and Mary eat too many peanuts they will become repulsive.

There are several ways to correct the mistake.

1. *Write them as two sentences.*
   1. Mabel flew down the stairs. She was in a hurry.
   2. John and Mary eat too many peanuts. They will become repulsive.
2. *Separate the two main* CLAUSES *with a* SEMICOLON.
   1. Mabel flew down the stairs; she was in a hurry.
   2. John and Mary eat too many peanuts; they will become repulsive.
3. *Join the two main clauses by a* CONJUNCTION (don't forget the comma).
   1. Mabel flew down the stairs, for she was in a hurry.
   2. John and Mary eat too many peanuts, and they will become repulsive.
4. *Put the ideas of one sentence into a subordinate* CLAUSE.
   1. Mabel flew down the stairs because she was in a hurry.
   2. If John and Mary eat too many peanuts, they will become repulsive.
   3. John and Mary, who eat too many peanuts, will become repulsive.
5. *Put the idea of one sentence into an* APPOSITIVE *phrase.*
   1. Mabel, a girl in a hurry, flew down the stairs.
   2. John and Mary, a couple who eat too many peanuts, will become repulsive.
6. *Turn one sentence into a participial* PHRASE.
   1. Being in a hurry, Mabel flew down the stairs.
   2. After eating too many peanuts, John and Mary will become repulsive.

semicolons (;)

A semicolon marks a greater degree of separation than a comma, not so great as a period. Use a semicolon between two CLAUSES not connected by conjunction but too closely related to call for a period.

Example:

John was on time; his girlfriend was late.

Use a semicolon to separate items in a series in which the items themselves contain commas.

Examples:

1. Maybelle saw a large, ugly dog; a friendly, intelligent pig; four of the cutest, quietest boys; and a monkey, whom she liked best.
2. To a hungry man, God is food; to a naked man, God is clothing; to a man without shelter, God is a house.

sentence fragments   see also SENTENCES.

Sentence fragments are pieces of sentences punctuated as if they were complete. Avoid them. The two most common kinds of sentence fragments are:

A. *Subordinate* CLAUSES *punctuated as sentences*

Examples:

1. Wrong: Because Perez could not see the ball.
2. Wrong: After she had been under water for three minutes.

These can be corrected in two ways.

1. Eliminating the subordinator will turn the expression into a complete sentence, but it will in all probability change the meaning somewhat.

132

Examples:

1. Perez could not see the ball.
2. She had been under water for three minutes.

2. Tie the fragment to a main clause.

Examples:

1. *Because Perez could not see the ball,* he struck out.
2. She was rescued *after she had been under water for three minutes.*

B. PARTICIPIAL PHRASES *punctuated as sentences*

Examples:

1. Disturbed by the eager crowds.
2. Hanging from the tree beside the house.

These, also, can be corrected in two ways:

1. Add a subject and AUXILIARY VERB.

Examples:

1. The horse was *disturbed by the eager crowds.*
2. A thousand bats were *hanging from the tree beside the house.*

2. Tie the fragment to a main clause.

Examples:

1. The horse was tense and irritable, *disturbed by the eager crowds.*
2. *Hanging from the tree beside the house,* the laundry swayed mysteriously.

sentence patterns   see SENTENCES, D.
sentence variety   see SENTENCES, E.
sentences

A sentence is a group of words that sounds complete.* You can easily tell which of the following word groups is a sentence and which is not.

---

*The traditional definition of a sentence is "a group of words that express a complete thought," but that definition doesn't work well because many sentences are not complete thoughts—for example, *Soon it started to do so again.*

1. that boy down the street
2. laughing in their soup, all the customers of the restaurant
3. my mother is a good cook
4. we give credit to those over eighty who are accompanied by their grandparents

The third and fourth examples sound complete. Read them again and see. They should be punctuated as sentences, beginning with a capital letter and ending with a period. But the first and second even sound incomplete. If you were reading them aloud, you would not end them with a pause and a drop in pitch (see RUN-ON SENTENCES). In the first example you also want to ask, "What about the boy down the street?" In the second you wonder, "What about all the customers?"

A. *Subject and predicate*

Sentences usually have two main parts, a *subject* and a *predicate*. The subject is the part about which something is said; the predicate says something about the subject.

Examples:

subject	predicate
1. George	coughed.
2. My little sister	has always been an awful pest.
3. Those men under the porch	think they are repairing the pipes.
4. We	remain too quiet in class.

The main word of the subject is called the *simple subject*. It is usually a NOUN or PRONOUN. All the words together in the subject are called the *complete subject*. The simple subjects in the four sentences just above are *George*, *sister*, *men*, and *we*. The main word or words in the predicate are the VERB or verb PHRASE, which can be called the *simple predicate*. The simple predicates in the four sentences are *coughed*, *has been*, *are repairing*, and *remain*.

Thus, the equation is: S + P = Sent.: subject plus predicate equals sentence. In other words, a sentence is the combination of a subject with a predicate in order to express a statement. Sentences are not the only proper mode of expression, of course. We often speak, and sometimes write, in nonsentences, especially when we answer questions in conversation. Further, there are thousands of ways of putting together sentences, as you know from your own listening and reading and speaking and writing.

B. *Run-on sentences and sentence fragments*

One of the main problems inexperienced writers encounter is *run-on sentences*—that is, sentences that are run together instead of being punctuated as separate sentences.

Example:

My mother loved turnips, she always made us eat them too.

For suggestions on correcting this problem, see RUN-ON SENTENCES.

Another major writing mistake is *sentence fragments*—parts of sentences punctuated as if they were complete sentences:

Examples:

1. John never got home for supper. *Because he had to stay late for practice.*
2. *Going down town on the bus.* We saw a holdup take place right on the sidewalk.

If you read the fragments aloud, you'll hear that they don't sound complete. For suggestions on correcting this problem, see SENTENCE FRAGMENTS.

C. *Four types of sentences*

Sentences are often classified into four main types, depending on the sort of response they will probably elicit from the reader or hearer.

1. *Statement sentences* (traditionally called *declarative sentences*) make a statement, give information, and so forth. Usually the response is continued attention or some such remark as "I see," "Yes?" or "Uh-

S

huh." Most of the sentences people use are statement sentences.

Examples:
1. Bears don't mind cold weather.
2. Music is the medicine of a troubled mind.
3. He wondered whether the grass was greener on the other side.

2. *Request sentences* (traditionally called *imperative sentences*) make a request or give an order. The expected response is some kind of action.

Examples:
1. Please follow that car.
2. Come in and eat before we both starve.
3. Kindly shut off the TV at once.
4. Get out.

Note that request sentences have no grammatical subject. We say that the subject is understood to be *"you."* "Please leave now" means, in effect, "You please leave now," for example.

3. *Question sentences* (traditionally called *interrogative sentences*) ask a question. The expected response is an answer.

Examples:
1. Did you hear the baby crying?
2. Who was that lady I saw you with last night?

Question sentences often begin with a *question word* (sometimes called an *interrogator* or an *interrogative pronoun*). Common question words are *who, why, when, what* and *where*—as in "*Who* did it?" "*Why* did he do it?"

Question sentences are formed from statement sentences in three ways.

a. By changing the order of the words so as to put the *simple subject* between the VERB and its AUXILIARY.

Example:

Statement: He *will go* tomorrow.

Question: *Will* he *go* tomorrow?

b. By adding a form of the verb *do* in front of the subject if there is no auxiliary in the statement.

Example:

Statement: He *likes* Mary.

Question: *Does* he *like* Mary?

c. By simply putting a *question mark* after a statement sentence.

Example:

Statement: I am handsome.

Question: I am handsome?

4. *Exclamatory sentences* express strong feeling. The expected response is any form of heightened attention—astonishment, disbelief, instant action, or some other.

Examples:

1. What a goof I made just before lunch!
2. How enormous your teeth are, Grandma!
3. Don't move or I'll shoot!

NOTES:

1. Sentences that begin with *what* or *how* and are not questions, as in the first two examples, are exclamatory sentences, even though *what* and *how* usually introduce question sentences.
2. Any sentence can be made exclamatory by ending it with an exclamation point.

D. *Sentence patterns*

There are four very common sentence patterns in English; most sentences are combinations, elaborations, expansions, and variations of these patterns. In each of the following, the *skeleton sentence*, the bare bones stripped of the flesh of MODIFIERS, has been underlined.

Pattern 1: (S V)	Subject	Verb
	1. Boys	fight.
	2. Those girls	wrestle fiercely.
	3. Their little dog	barked loudly all night.

137

S

Pattern 2:	*Subject*	*Verb*	*Direct Object*
(S V DO)			
	1. <u>Boys</u>	<u>admire</u>	<u>heroes</u>.
	2. Some <u>girls</u>	<u>detest</u>	<u>sewing</u>.
	3. That silly <u>child</u>	<u>broke</u>	my <u>arm</u> yesterday.

Pattern 3:	*Subject*	*Linking Verb*	*Noun Complement*
(S LV NC)			
	1. <u>Boys</u>	<u>are</u>	<u>people</u>.
	2. That <u>girl</u>	<u>is</u>	an <u>expert</u>.
	3. My fierce <u>hound</u>	suddenly <u>became</u>	a neigh-borhood <u>menace</u>.

Pattern 4:	*Subject*	*Linking Verb*	*Adjective Complement*
(S LV AdjC)			
	1. <u>Boys</u>	<u>are</u>	<u>creative</u>.
	2. That <u>girl</u>	<u>looks</u>	<u>stronger</u> than the boys.
	3. The first <u>problem</u>	<u>was</u> always	<u>difficult</u> last year.

Summary: 1. S V
2. S V DO
3. S LV NC
4. S LV AdjC

S

E. *Sentence variety*

A piece of writing in which the SENTENCES are repeatedly of the same sort and length is likely to make dull reading. As you write, think about variety, about how your writing sounds. (Writing has a sound even when it is read silently.) After you have written your paper, read it aloud to hear again how it sounds. Revise it if it is monotonous (see REVISION OF PAPERS). Consider varying the way your sentences begin. Start some with a single-word MODIFIER, some with a PHRASE, some with a subordinate CLAUSE. Vary the length and shape of your sentences. However, don't drag in a phrase or a subordinate clause just because you haven't used one for a while. Such an easy out will probably just make your writing sound stilted or artificial. Have confidence in your inner ear, but *keep it listening.*

F. *Simple, compound, and complex sentences*

1. A *simple sentence* has only one independent main CLAUSE and no subordinate clauses.

Example:

Galahad went for a walk Saturday afternoon.

2. A *compound sentence* is composed of two sentences joined by a CONJUNCTION. A COMMA precedes the conjunction.

Example:

Galahad went crazy in the afternoon, but Mabel remained stable.

> NOTE: A simple sentence with a compound VERB does not take a comma before the conjunction.
> *Example:*
> Galahad *went* crazy in the afternoon but
> (verb)
> *calmed* down that night. [*calmed down that*
> (verb)
> *night* is not a sentence]

3. A *complex sentence* is composed of a main clause and a subordinate clause. If the subordinate clause begins the sentence, set it off with a comma.

Examples:
1. James was extremely hungry because he hadn't eaten since midnight.
2. Because he hadn't eaten since midnight, James gnawed on the table leg.

See also RUN-ON SENTENCES; SENTENCE FRAGMENTS.

series

Use commas to separate items in a series—words, PHRASES, subordinate CLAUSES, or short SENTENCES.

Examples:

Words

We sat, ate, burped, talked, and left.

Zerilda saw her mother, the dog, and three mice enter the garage.

It was a gloomy, wretched, fearsome house.

Phrases

Those beasts hunted around the garbage pail, under the house, behind the fence, and among the lilacs.

Subordinate Clauses

Josh insists on knowing why I talk, when I talk, with whom I talk, and whether I say anything.

Short Sentences

My brother washed the car, Dad swept the garage, Mom cleaned the livingroom, and I wrote poetry.

NOTES:
1. It is not always necessary to put a comma before "and" unless omitting it would make the meaning unclear. However, using a comma before "and" is never incorrect.
2. When a noun is modified by two or more words and there's no pause as you read them, don't use commas to separate them: "It was a fine old brick house." (You can test whether you need the commas by seeing if changing the order of the modifiers will still sound sensible. If it won't, don't

use commas. "It was a brick old fine house" sounds wrong, so don't use commas in the original sentence. "It was a strange, ancient, decaying house" needs commas because no matter what order you put the modifiers in, the sentence still sounds sensible: "It was a decaying, ancient, strange house." (See MODIFIERS.)

See also SEMICOLONS, 2.

short stories

There are hundreds of ways to write good short stories (stories that are only a few pages long, much shorter than NOVELS) and no foolproof formula that will insure success. Most short stories share certain characteristics, however, and it is helpful to a beginning writer to know them.

A. *Characters and problem*

A story centers on what happens to a person or people (the characters) who face a problem. In a good story the characters and problems will seem real in some way. Even a fantasy will have a sort of reality about it, even though it could never actually happen.

B. *Plot*

The events of a story fit together into a plot, or plan, which gives the story a point and a sense of direction. The reader's interest in the plot development is called *suspense*. Most stories keep the reader in some sort of suspense.

C. *Resolution*

The characters in a short story "solve" their problem in a sequence called the resolution. At the beginning of the story the reader's curiosity is aroused; by the end it is somehow satisfied. The story will probably leave the reader with something to think about. The resolution may definitely be a happy or unhappy one, or it may involve an insoluble problem, the resolution lying in what the character learns about himself or others.

D. *Setting*

Most stories have a setting—the physical place

or places in which the events take place. The setting may be described at or near the beginning or it may be developed as the plot unfolds.

E. *Beginning*

Since a short story is short, it usually has a beginning that quickly grabs the interest of the reader. The five examples that follow are by well-known authors.

"I See You Never," by Ray Bradbury

The soft knock came at the kitchen door, and when Mrs. O'Brian opened it, there on the back porch were her best tenant, Mr. Ramirez, and two police officers, one on each side of him. Mr. Ramirez just stood there, walled in and small.

"Why, Mr. Ramirez!" said Mrs. O'Brian.

"A Wicked Boy," by Anton Chekhov

Ivan Ivanych Lapkin, a young man of nice appearance, and Anna Semionovna, a young girl with a little turned-up nose, went down the steep bank and sat down on a small bench. The bench stood right by the water among some thick young osier bushes. What a wonderful little place! Once you'd sat down, you were hidden from the world—only the fish saw you, and the watertigers, running like lightning over the water.

"The Upturned Face," by Stephen Crane

"What will we do now?" said the adjutant, troubled and excited.

"Bury him," said Timothy Lean.

The two officers looked down close to their toes where lay the body of their comrade. The face was chalk-blue; gleaming eyes stared at the sky. Over the two upright figures was a windy sound of bullets. . . .

"Truth and Consequences," by Brendan Gill

She had straight blond hair and a red mouth, and she was lame. Every day she played golf and went swimming in the center of a crowd of boys. Charles, sitting with his mother on the hotel porch, watched her and nodded while his mother repeated, "Isn't it extraordinary, a girl like that? I wonder what in the world they see in her."

"The Hour of Letdown," by E. B. White

When the man came in, carrying the machine, most of us looked up from our drinks, because we had never seen anything like it before. The man set the thing down on top of the bar near the beerpulls. It took up an ungodly amount of room and you could see the bartender didn't like it any too well, having this big, ugly-looking gadget parked right there.

"Two rye-and-water," the man said.

F. *Truth*

Although a short story is fiction (that is, the events didn't really happen), it is usually true in that it shows something about human life and experience. In many ways authors of fiction can convey more truths than can authors of nonfiction because they are free to select whatever experience they wish in order to show their truth, and they do not have to worry about embarrassing themselves or other people who exist in real life.

In recent years some writers have departed from the model of the short story and experimented with stories that have little obvious form, stories which do not appear to begin or end in any structured way. They may be a slice of life, a stream of fantasy, or a congeries of events and impressions.

similes   see FIGURATIVE LANGUAGE, A.

simple sentences   see SENTENCES, F.

simple subject   see SENTENCES, A.

singular   see PLURAL.

speech   see LANGUAGE.

speech-making

Speech-making is a useful skill—both in school and college, where you may be assigned the task, and also later in life, if you are a person who is likely to hold positions of responsibility in which you will need to inform, persuade, or entertain people.

1. In making a speech, as in writing an ESSAY or composition, the most important requirement for success is to have something interesting that you want to say (see also ESSAYS, B; REPORTS, 1).

2. Since you must hold the attention of your listeners, it is also important that your speech be well organized, so that they can follow your ideas very easily as you go from one part of your speech to the next. It is more difficult for a listener to follow an organizational pattern than it is for a reader, since the listener cannot look back. Your pattern of organization must therefore be easily understood. After an interest-provoking introduction, you may even want to say, as you would not be likely to do in writing, something on the order of "I shall be talking to you about [whatever your subject is] in four parts; I will then draw a couple of conclusions which I hope will convince you."

3. It is rare that a person can read a speech well. The text comes between the speaker and the listeners. On the other hand, memorizing the speech, unless it comes easily to you, is often not satisfactory because the speech will sound memorized and the audience may feel nervous that the speaker will forget his words (but see MEMORIZATION). For most people the best method is to speak from a clear outline that contains key words to keep the flow steady but leaves the actual words of each sentence up to the speaker to form as he or she proceeds, guided by the outline (see OUTLINING). An example of such an outline follows at the end of this entry.

4. It is an advantage of working from an outline

that you can look at your listeners as you speak, and they feel that you are talking directly to them with words spoken just for them. It is very important to look at different people in the audience as you speak.

5. Some people use a formal style of speech, others prefer a more casual one. Your personality, your subject, and the nature and size of your audience will help you determine the proper style. If you're formal, don't be stiff; if you're casual, don't slouch or wander.

6. Obviously, to succeed, a speech must be easy to hear—be *audible*. If there is no microphone and public-address system, be sure to *speak to the back row*. If you keep the back row in mind, your voice will almost automatically reach the entire audience audibly. Some speakers mumble and then look up and say loudly to the back, "Can you hear me back there?" to which the answer is, at that moment, "Yes." Satisfied, they go back to mumbling.

If there is a microphone, it is best for most speakers to stand a couple of feet away from it, to speak across it to the audience. However, speaking close to the mike in a confidential sort of way can be effective, provided you stay close and don't overwhelm it with a loud voice or strong breathing. If you're showing slides, don't turn away from the mike as you point out the pictures. A small neck mike that can be clipped on a few inches below your chin is convenient if you have to move about during your speech.

7. If possible, use a lectern to hold your notes. A simple music stand will do; whatever you use ought to be high enough to let you switch your eyes easily from notes to audience and back. If you have to hold your notes in your

hands (and cards are better than sheets of paper; they don't shake and rattle), frankly hold them in front of you so that you can easily keep track of where you are.

8. You really do need to be conscious of your body. Otherwise you may sway back and forth, scratch your head, swing your arms, or make meaningless repetitive gestures. The best thing is to hold your body at ease but rather still. Use your hands and arms to make gestures, perhaps for emphasis or to indicate size or feeling; but do not gesture excessively. All unnecessary body movements—especially repeated ones—distract your listeners.

9. If you come to the end of a point and need to refer briefly to your notes, simply do it. You don't have to say "uh." If you are stuck for a word, wait until it comes to you; no "uh" is necessary. A moment of silence does no. harm at all; in fact, silence often focuses the audience's attention on you.

10. Unless you are an experienced speaker, you should practice your speech by yourself. If you can manage it, you might practice it before some members of your family or with friends to get their suggestions.

11. While practicing, time your speech. *Never* go over your time limit. Novice speakers quite often find that when they finally deliver their speeches, they go faster than in practice, probably because they are nervous. Many speakers speak too fast.

12. If you practice in the same room in which you will eventually make your speech, remember that a room full of people absorbs sound and that people, even when they are interested, move about and rustle a little. You need to speak more loudly than in an empty room.

13. Two problems facing some speakers are getting started and getting stopped. Therefore, it is good insurance to memorize your first sentence and last sentence. Speak them looking right at the listeners, not sounding memorized, and you'll be guaranteed a confident start and finish.

14. The following is a sample set of notes for a speech entitled "Living in a Large Family." Notice that the first and last memorized sentences are written out and that the organization of the speech is clearly evident; but most of the outline is made up of key words or phrases that suggest whole sentences or paragraphs that will be spoken extemporaneously (not memorized):

John Krim

LIVING IN A LARGE FAMILY

I. Introduction

Living in a large family—like mine—may not be peaceful, but I like it, because if you can stay alive, you're prepared for almost any problem you may meet in the future.

Here are several problems:

II. Getting attention
   A. Everyone needs it
   B. Maybe in small family you get more, but—
      1. too easy—
            parents foresee every problem
      2. practically no privacy—
            just *you* are the focus
   C. Large family—have to *earn* it! how?
      1. accomplishing something *good*
         a. my model car
         b. repair cellar steps
      2. do something terribly *bad*
         a. stole a quarter
         b. locked sister in room

3. have really severe problem
   a. teacher who hated me
   b. neighborhood boy beat me up
      BUT ...
4. in between you live your own life: *good*! self-reliance

III. Getting money
   A. Everyone needs it too! (like attention)
   B. In large family, unless rich, supply is limited
      1. no automatic allowance
      2. you have to *earn* it
         a. how I did
         b. benefits
            (1) ——
            (2) ——
                .
                .
                .
                .
                .

VIII. Conclusion
   Thus you can see that although life is harder in a large family, it is better because (1) you learn to get what you need and thus are prepared for life, and (2) you have lots of privacy, more than if you were the center of your parents' attention.

Announcements

A special kind of speech is the announcement. Its main purpose is to convey information. Unless you are trying for some special effects, the best way to make announcements is to follow a few rules.

1. Wait to start until the audience is quiet. If they don't quiet down until after you start, start again.
2. Speak slowly, clearly, and to the back row.
3. State the essential information at the beginning (what? when? where? for whom? how much?) and repeat it at the end. Give not only the date, but also the day of the week: "Wednesday, March 11," for example.

spelling

Good spelling in English has little to do with IQ scores or intelligence. You can be quite dull and spell well or brilliant and spell poorly. But unfortunately many people mistakenly believe that people who spell poorly are stupid or are badly educated. This is one reason for learning to spell as correctly as you can. Another is that correct spelling makes your writing easier to understand.

Naturally good spellers have few problems. When they need to write a word, they "see" it correctly in their minds and copy it from their mental image. They can tell if it looks right once they've written it. If it's a word they don't know, they look it up in a dictionary and study it to establish a mental image. For such people, with good visual memories, spelling is a nearly effortless process.

But most people have to work at becoming acceptable spellers. And the nature of the English language, which is full of exceptions, makes the job harder. There are often several ways of spelling words wrong that sound right.

An effective method for learning to spell words that are difficult for you follows.

1. When you are not sure how to spell a word, look it up, or ask someone who knows to *write it down* for you. *Then learn it at once—* don't just copy it. If you do, you'll only have to look it up again the next time. Once you have the correct spelling—the model—in front of you:

    a. Look at it and pronounce it.

    b. Underline each SYLLABLE.

    c. Say it several times, syllable by syllable; then pronounce the entire word.

    d. Be aware of any trouble spots in the word.

    e. When you've got the word in mind, cover the model and write the word down.

f. Check your spelling with the model. If you got it wrong, start over.

g. Now write the word on your paper. (Also write it on the appropriate blank alphabetical page in this book or in a notebook.) Try to write the word again a couple of times during the next day or two.

2. Learn all the words you misspell on your papers or other assignments. These are *your* problems, more important for you than any list of words in a speller.

3. Learn the six SPELLING RULES. They will help you spell certain groups of words that involve major spelling problems.

4. Learn the SPELLING DEMONS. These are words often used and often misspelled.

5. Keep a list of words you have learned. You may do this on the blank pages at the end of each letter section of this book or in a notebook. Record each word in a phrase or sentence if necessary to show its meaning. [*"It's* a nice day." *"Its* roof blew off."] From time to time go over your list of words to refresh your memory. When you write the words, try to think of MNEMONIC DEVICES to aid you.

spelling demons

The expression "spelling demons" is applied to words that are often used and often misspelled. After many of them in the list that follows I have indicated a way to help you remember the correct spelling. It will help you to underline the SYLLABLES to clarify how to pronounce the word and how it breaks into spellable parts. When a phrase is given along with a word, learn it, since usually the problem is not how to spell the word, but *which* of several possible spellings—with different meanings—to use.

A good way to master this list is to have someone test you on the words in groups of twenty-five. Mark the ones you missed or were unsure of (even though you may have guessed corectly), learn them, and take the test again. Then go on to the next group of twenty-five. When you've completed the list of words, take a summary test on all the words you missed or were not sure of, to be certain you still know them. When you take a test, always have the words dictated to you in a sentence, and do not have the other person say them in a way that hints at the correct spelling.

If there are other demon words for you, add them to the list. *Don't* waste time studying words you already know.

175 Spelling Demons

1. absent   absence
2. accept (ac + cept)—"*accept* an invitation"
3. accommodate (two *c*'s, two *m*'s)
4. across (one *c*)
5. affect—"How does it *affect* you?"
6. again (a + gain)
7. all right (always two words)
8. already
9. among (a + mong)
10. angle—"a sharp *angle*"
11. answer (note the *w*)
12. apparent—"Many things are *apparent* to a *parent*."
13. appear   appearance (two *p*'s; ends in *-ance*)
14. argument (*e* is dropped from *argue*)
15. athletics (only three syllables—ath + let + ics)
16. author (ends in *-or*)
17. beginner   beginning (two *n*'s)
18. belief   believe (*ie*)
19. business (*sin* in bu*sin*ess)
20. busy
21. calendar (ends in *-dar*)
22. capital (a *capital* letter)

23. capitol (the building with a dome)
24. captain (ends in *-tain*)
25. character (*ch* and two *a*'s)
26. choose—"Now I *choose* you."   chose—
    "Yesterday I *chose* her."
27. clothes—"I wear *clothes*."
28. color (ends in *-or*)
29. column (note the *n*, as in *columnar*)
30. coming (one *m*)
31. committee (double *m*, double *t*, double *e*)
32. completely (complete + ly)
33. conscience (*con* + *science*) conscientious
34. conscious (*sci* + *ous*)
35. control   controlled
36. council (student council, a group)
37. counsel (means advice or to advise)
38. counselor or counsellor (both are correct)
39. country
40. course (the English *course*; of *course*)
41. criticism   criticize (critic + *ism* or *ize*)
42. deceive (*cei*; see SPELLING RULES, 1)
43. decided
44. definitely (de + *finite* + ly)
45. description (*de* + script)
46. develop   development (no *e* after the *p*)
47. different (differ + *ent*)
48. disappear (dis + appear)
49. disappointed (dis + appointed)
50. discipline
51. doctor—"Call the doct*or or* else!"
52. doesn't (does + n't)
53. effect—"a beautiful *effect*"; "to *effect* a
    change"
54. embarrassed (double *r*, double *s*)
55. emphasize—"Emphasize its *size*."
56. equipment (equip + ment) equipped
57. exaggerate (two *g*'s, one *r*)
58. excellent (*-ent*)

59. except—"I like it *except* for the dirt"; an *except*ion
60. experience (four syllables: ex + per + i + ence)
61. explanation (the *i* is dropped from *explain*)
62. extremely (extreme + ly)
63. familiar (ends in -*liar*)
64. February "Say 'BR!' in Fe*br*uary."
65. finally (final + ly; three syllables)
66. foreign foreigner (*ei*)
67. forty
68. fourth—"third and fourth"
69. friend—"a fri*end* to the *end*"
70. general generally (Pronounce all the syllables: gen + er + al + ly.)
71. government (govern + ment)
72. governor (govern + or)
73. grammar—"Bad gram*mar* will *mar*."
74. guess (note the *u*)
75. height (ends in *t*)
76. humorous (hum*o*r + ous)
77. immediately (contains *ate* + *ly*)
78. independent independence (*ent*, *ence*)
79. interesting (in + ter + est + ing)
80. its—"in *its* place" (possessive pronoun)
81. it's—"*It's* here." (it is)
82. knew—"He *knew* the answer."
83. know—"I *know* him."
84. laid—"Today the hen lays an egg; yesterday she *laid* nothing."
85. lead (means both a heavy metal and to act as leader)
86. led—"He *led* like a leader."
87. library (note: *br*)
88. license
89. loose—"a *loose* bolt"
90. lose losing—"He is losing his way."
91. marriage (marri + age)
92. mathematics (math + e + mat + ics)

93. meant (mean + t)
94. medicine (note: *dic*)
95. minute (ends in *-ute*)
96. misspell (mis + spell)
97. motor (ends in *-or*)
98. naturally (natural + ly)
99. necessary   necessarily (one *c*; two *s*'s)
100. notice   noticeable   noticing
101. occasion (two *c*'s; one *s*)
102. occurred   occurring (two *c*'s; two *r*'s; see SPELLING RULES, 3)
103. omitted (one *m*; two *t*'s)
104. opinion (ends in *-ion*)
105. opportunity (p*o*r)
106. paid—"Now I pay; then I *paid*."
107. parallel
108. passed—"She *passed* the exam; he *passed* her on the street."
109. past—"*past* and present"
110. perhaps (per + haps)
111. personal—"a private, *personal* matter"
112. personnel—"the *personnel* in the office"
113. piece—"a *piece* of *pie*"
114. pleasant (ends in *-ant*)
115. precede—"one *precedes* two" (goes before it)
116. prepare   preparation
117. principal (the principal—main—idea) "The princi*pal* is my *pal*."
118. principle—"It's a good princip*le* [ru*le*] to tell the truth."
119. privilege—"Pri*vile*ge is *vile*."
120. probably (pro*bab*ly)
121. proceed—"Please *proceed* slowly." procedure (one *e*)
122. professor (one *f*; ends in *-or*)
123. quiet (two syllables)—"a *quiet* place"
124. realize (real + ize; to make real)
125. really (real + ly)

126. receipt (note: *pt*)
127. receive (*cei*; see SPELLING RULES, 1)
128. recommend (re + commend)
129. refer   referring
130. religious
131. repetition (note: *pet*)
132. restaurant
133. rhythm (r*hyth*m: two *h*'s, two syllables)
134. safety (safe + ty)
135. schedule
136. seize (*sei*)
137. sense—"That makes *sense*." (two *s*'s)
     sensible
138. separate (*a rat* in sep*arat*e)
139. similar (ends in -*lar*)
140. sincerely (sincere + ly)
141. speech (two *e*'s; *not* like sp*eak*)
142. studying (stud + y + ing; three syllables)
143. succeed (double *c*; double *e*)
144. success (double *c*; double *s*)
145. surely (sure + ly)
146. surprise (sur + prise)
147. suspense (three *s*'s)
148. than—"larger *than* mine" (normally
     pronounced th'n)
149. their—"*their* house" (possessive pronoun)
150. there—"*There* are two." "*Here* and *there*."
151. therefore (ends in -*e*)
152. they're—"*They're* gone." (*they are*)
153. thoroughly (thor + ough + ly)
154. though—"strong, though small"
155. threw—"I *threw* him out."
156. through—"Go *through* the door."
157. to—"*to* go"; "*to* the store"
158. together—"They went *together to get her*."
159. too—"*too* much"; "me *too*" (means *also*)
160. tragedy—"There is *age* in tr*age*dy."
161. tried
162. truly (note: the *e* is dropped)

163. Tuesday
164. two—"One plus one equals *two*."
165. until
166. usually unusually (Get all the syllables: un + us + u + al + ly.)
167. valuable (val + u + a + ble)
168. weather—"stormy *weather*"
169. Wednesday (Wed + nes + day)
170. whether—"*whether* or not"
171. who's—"Who's on first?" (means *who is*)
172. whose—"*Whose* is it?" (possessive pronoun)
173. woman (*wo + man*, singular; *wo + men*, plural)
174. writing (one *t*; based on *write*) written
175. (the longest word in the English language) pneumonoultramicroscopicsilicovolcanoconiosis

spelling rules

There are a great many spelling rules. Here are the six that I think are useful enough to learn; and even they won't be useful to everyone. Some people know how to apply rules; others never seem to be able to learn. If you can learn, though, each rule will help you deal with a whole group of problem words and situations. Don't try to memorize the rules word for word. Instead, understand the spelling problem each rule deals with. *Do* memorize the exceptions.

Rule 1: *ie* or *ei*

a. When sound is *ee*.

Put *i* before *e* [believe] except after *c* [receive, ceiling]

b. When sound is not *ee*.

Put *e* before *i* [height, weight]

Exception:

The important exceptions to this rule can be remembered easily if you learn two sentences.

1. He s*ei*zed (n)*ei*ther w*ei*rd l*ei*sure. [Contains *ei* words pronounced *ee*.]

156

2. His fr*ie*nd s*ie*ved the misch*ie*f. [Contains *ie* words not pronounced *ee.*]

Rule 2: words ending in silent *e*

a. Words that end in silent *e* [taste, hope, nerve, remove] usually drop the final *e* before a suffix beginning with a vowel [-ing, -ed, -ous, -able].

Examples:

tasting, hoped, nervous, removable.

Exceptions:

Exceptions are words ending in *-ce* and *-ge,* which with suffixes produce words such as "noticeable" and "courageous." The *e* keeps the *c* and the *g* soft.

b. Words that end in silent *e* usually keep the *e* before a suffix beginning with a consonant (-ment, -ly, -ful, -ness, -less).

Examples:

excitement, lonely, careless.

Exceptions:

Three common exceptions are: His *ninth judgment* was *truly* wrong.

Rule 3: Doubling the final consonant

When one-syllable words [hit, stop, put] and words accented on the last syllable [re*mit,* con*trol,* oc*cur*] end in a single consonant after a single vowel, the final consonant is doubled when a suffix beginning with a vowel [-er, -ed, -ing, -able, -ible, -ence, -ance] is added.

Examples:

hit, hitter; stop, stopped; put, putting; control, controllable; occur, occurred; remit, remittance.

Exceptions:

Not included in this rule are:

a. Words having two vowels before the single consonant [s*ea*t, s*ea*ted].

b. Words ending in two consonants [resu*lt*, re-su*lt*ing].

c. Words not accented on the last syllable [*o*pen, *o*pened; *ben*efit, *ben*efiting].

S

Rule 4: Plurals and third person singulars of words ending in *y* following a consonant

Nouns that end in *y* with a consonant before it (examples: baby, lady, sky) form their plurals by changing the *y* to *i* and adding *es* (examples: babies, ladies, skies).

Verbs that end in *y* with a consonant before them (examples: try, cry, reply) form their third person singulars by changing the *y* to *i* and adding *es* or *ed* (examples: tries, tried; cries, cried; replies, replied).

Rule 5: Adding suffixes to words ending in *y*

1. Words that end in *y* after a consonant change the *y* to *i* before any suffix except *-ing*.

Examples:

plenty + ful = plentiful
ready + ness = readiness
merry + ment = merriment
steady + est = steadiest
happy + er = happier
rely + able = reliable

2. When the suffix is *-ing*, the *y* is unchanged [try, trying; study, studying]. Pronouncing these words carefully will help: "stud + y + ing"—three syllables.

Rule 6: PREFIXES

Prefixes [mis-, dis-, over-, re-, un-] are added to *root* words without changing the spelling of the prefix or the root word.

Examples:

misspell, disagree, overdue, reinvest, unnecessary, disappear, dissolve.

stories   SEE SHORT STORIES.

study skills

How to "study" is not a simple lesson, easily taught. Each person has his or her style of learning. There are, however, some routines and practices that are helpful to many people and that may help you.

1. *Write down your assignments*, including the date due, clearly, promptly, in a regular place, preferably a small homework notebook, not on just any available scrap of paper. If you aren't sure what the assignment means, ask the teacher.

2. *Have a regular schedule for home study*. Most people work better after dinner than before. When you return from school, your mind needs a rest, and your body requires some food and exercise. However, styles and rhythms of brainwork and bodywork differ.

3. *Have a regular place for study*, equipped with pencils, pen, paper, scissors, ruler, dictionary, calendar, and a good lamp. Occasionally, though, an escape from the regular place can provide new inspiration—under a tree? on the roof?

4. *Be certain of the purpose of an assignment before you do it*. Ask yourself, "What am I supposed to learn from this? Why was it assigned to me?" Teachers usually have a particular goal in mind when they give an assignment. What is it? If you don't know, ask—tactfully.

5. *Skim over any reading assignment rapidly before reading it closely*. Glance at the main headings and titles, or paragraph beginnings, to get a general idea of what it's about and to help you relate the ideas to the main topic and to the rest of the course.

6. *Use any study aids in the book*. Note the chapter title and the headings of the main sections. If there are italicized words, read them with special care. Look closely at any numbered lists of points. Be sure you know why the authors included any charts, maps, and pictures. Go over any questions and exercises at the end of the chapter; they will usually stress the main ideas.

7. *Pause after each paragraph or section of the book to see if you can recall the main ideas*. If you cannot, reread the passage. Pausing for recall and review is one of the best ways to fix the ideas in your mind.

8. *Mark your book if you own it.* Reading should be an active process. Don't just settle back and let the words come into your eyes and be absorbed into a sort of mental fog. Instead, read with a pencil or colored marker in hand and make circles, underlinings, squiggles, and the like, to emphasize main points.

9. *Look up new words if necessary.* Always keep a dictionary at your place of study. After you've looked up a word, try to use it a couple of times within a day or so to implant it in your mind. However, don't do so much looking up that it breaks the train of thought of the passage (see VOCABULARY BUILDING).

10. *When you've finished an assignment, think back and try to recall the main ideas.* This is a quick way to fix the ideas in your mind and to show where you need to reread. Don't just heave a sigh of relief and close the book when you reach the last word. Try to answer any end-of-chapter questions. If you cannot, review the appropriate section.

11. Remember, there are *different kinds of reading* for different kinds of assignments. Get your mind set for the kind of reading you think applies (see READING).

12. *Note and study all corrections and suggestions made to you in class and on your papers.* If your teacher makes a correction on your paper or a suggestion to you in class, that's important. *Note also any suggestion made to the class in general.* If the teacher thinks something is worth taking time to mention particularly, it's probably important (at least for the course), and teachers have a way of emphasizing what they are likely to ask for on a later test.

13. *Plan your time* on any long-term assignment. If you have three weeks to do a report, divide up your time, perhaps spending a week doing rough organization and collecting materials, another week reading and taking notes, and a third week reorganizing and writing up your report and proofreading it.

14. *While doing an assignment, note down any*

points about which you are not clear and bring them up in class at the beginning of the next period. This is not only a good way to learn; it also makes a wonderful impression on the teacher.

15. *Learn to make a rough outline* (see OUTLINING).

16. *When reviewing for tests, don't reread all the materials.* Instead, use the study aids in the book, the marks you have made, and any notes you may have taken on your reading or on what the teacher has emphasized. You may take notes on your notes or mark them up further to summarize them. Spend your time on the parts you don't know (see REVIEWING FOR TESTS AND EXAMS).

17. *Your basic obligation to your work is to try your best and be interested in it.* Try not to set up a block between you and your education by saying that you're bored or feeling that the work is "stupid." You have a perfect right to your feelings, but if you let them control your actions, you may fail to learn. Instead, strive to find something in the work that can catch your interest.

See also READING.

subject(ive) case   see CASES; PRONOUNS.

subjects

The subject is one of the two main parts of most SENTENCES. It is the part about which something is said.

Examples:

1. *My idea of happiness* is four feet on a fire-
(subject)
place fender. (O. W. HOLMES)

2. *Few horses* go as fast as the money you bet on
(subject)
them.

3. *He who hesitates* gets bumped from the rear.
(subject)
(HOMER PHILLIPS)

S

4. *It* looks like a dying panda.
   (subject)

5. Chirping bravely under the tractor was *a small cricket*.
   (subject)

The main part of a sentence other than the subject is the PREDICATE.

The main word in the complete subject is called the *simple subject*: *idea, horses, he, it,* and *cricket* in the five sentences above.

subjects and predicates   see SENTENCES, A.

subject-verb agreement   see AGREEMENT OF SUBJECT AND VERB.

subordinate clauses, subordinators   see CLAUSES, B.

subordinating conjunctions   see CLAUSES, B.

suffixes

Suffixes are words or parts of words added to the end of words or word roots to change or add to the meaning or to change the TENSE. Knowing certain common suffixes, most of them borrowed or inherited from Greek or Latin, will help you make intelligent guesses about the meanings of words you may not know. Some common suffixes follow.

suffix	meaning	examples in word
-ant	one who (is)	servant, inhabitant
-er	(does)	buyer, creeper
-ist	(believes in)	typist, deist
-or	one who does	bettor, operator
-ful	characterized by: full of	beautiful, remorseful
-ic	like	fantastic, demonic
-ish	like	impish, foolish
-ize	to cause to become	standardize, popularize

suffix	meaning	examples in word
-less	without	hopeless, shapeless
-ly	in the manner	quietly, disgustingly
-sion ⎫ -tion ⎭	process of or state of being	⎧ expulsion, rejection, ⎩ depression
-ward	in the direction of	homeward, earthward
-hood ⎫ -ness ⎭	condition of	⎧ childhood, ⎪ priesthood ⎨ foolishness, ⎩ pretentiousness

Suffixes are listed in dictionaries, usually in small capitals enclosed in brackets ([ ]) after the definition of a word as separate entries (usually preceded by a hyphen, as "-hood").

See PREFIXES for a comparison of the functions of prefixes and suffixes.

syllabication

Syllabication is the division of words into syllables. A syllable is a word or parts of a word that is uttered as a single vocal impulse.

Since the rules of syllabication are complicated, the only way to be certain how a word is syllabized is to refer to a DICTIONARY. Pronouncing a word aloud carefully will often enable you to make an intelligent guess.

When a word must be divided at the end of a line, divide it between syllables (see HYPHENS). A word can be divided between double consonants usually (dif ference; Mis sis sip pi). Never divide a one-syllable word.

symbols to guide revision of papers

It saves time for you and the teacher if you agree on a set of symbols to be used when your paper is read and marked (see REVISION OF PAPERS). What follows is a set of comonly accepted and useful symbols. Each symbol in the margin means that there is a particular problem to be corrected in the line of writing beside it.

S

awk	awkwardly expressed, If you are unable to understand what the awkward construction is, consult your teacher.
cap	begin the word with a capital letter.
comb	combine into one sentence as you judge best.
frag	SENTENCE FRAGMENT—a group of words punctuated as a sentence but not a sentence. Change it by making it into a sentence or, more commonly, combining it with the sentence that precedes or follows it.
gr	mistake in GRAMMAR.
H	handwriting unclear.
lc	lower case. You should not have used a capital letter.
M?	meaning is unclear or not what you intended.
note	note a suggestion or change made in the text.
O	order of words is wrong or poor and needs changing.
¶	new PARAGRAPH is needed here.
no ¶	you should not start a new paragraph here.
p	punctuation error [p(;)—use a SEMICOLON; p(-)—use a HYPHEN, and so on].
ref	what does the word refer to? Usually means unclear PRONOUN REFERENCE.
rep	awkward repetition.
r-o	RUN-ON SENTENCES—two or more sentences run together. Should be punctuated as separate sentences or otherwise revised.
sp	error in SPELLING.
T	error in TENSE.
W	wrong word—choose a better one.
w.o.	write out; do not use ABBREVIATION or figure (see NUMBERS).
⨍	delete (omit). [Examples: The ~~big~~ large boy coughed. Come ~~here!~~]
/	divide into two words [the main|street].
⌒	join into one word [road‿block].

164

;/	insert the punctuation where indicated—in this case, a semicolon.
?	is this what you mean? Are you sure of your facts? Clarify the text.
∧	something is omitted; supply it.
	[Two plus ∧ equals four.]
X	obvious error.

See also REVISION OF PAPERS.

_____

_____

_____

_____

_____

_____

_____

_____

_____

_____

_____

_____

_____

S

table of contents   see BOOKS.

taking tests and exams

If you can excel in a test or examination, even though you may not have done as well as you'd like to in your daily work, you can greatly improve your record. More important, reviewing intelligently is an excellent way to learn the material of a course, and the thinking and writing under pressure that is required during a test or exam may be good training for such challenges in the future.

A. *Preparing for the test*

There are many ways to prepare, and you should develop one that suits your style and that works for you. See REVIEWING FOR TESTS AND EXAMS for specific suggestions that may help you.

B. *Taking the test*

Again, in taking tests styles differ and people succeed in different ways. The following practices work well for many.

1. Look over the entire test quickly before you start answering any of the questions. If there are essay questions, read them right away so that your mind can mull over them even as you are working on other parts of the test. Jot down (with key words) various points to avoid losing ideas you had at first reading.

2. Bring a watch and plan your time. Don't spend more time than you should on any question. Usually the proportion of time allotted to a question should be related to the proportion of credit given for it. Leave

167

some blank space at the end of each answer in case you have time to come back to it at the end to add more information.

3. Read the directions and questions carefully. Many a person has failed or done poorly on a test or exam by misinterpreting the directions or, in effect, answering the wrong question because he misread it.

4. Write legibly but not too slowly. *Never* waste time copying over an answer on a timed test.

5. Be sure that you number your answers plainly according to the numbers of the questions. Make it easy for the teacher to follow your paper.

6. Answer first the questions you know best (but don't spend more than the allotted portion of time on them) and do the hardest ones last—unless, of course, you are required to answer the questions in order. Never spend a lot of time puzzling uselessly over a question you cannot answer. Come back to it at the end if there's time.

7. Unless you're a sure writer, save a few minutes (maybe 5 percent of the time) to PROOFREAD and revise your answers.

8. If you're not certain of an answer, make intelligent guesses. This practice is especially important on multiple-choice tests. If you can eliminate one or more of the choices as certainly wrong, it will pay you to guess among the others.

See also REVIEWING FOR TESTS AND EXAMS.

tenses

Tense, in grammar, refers to time, and the tense of a sentence is usually expressed by the VERB. Tenses can be divided roughly into three large categories: present, past, and future. There are many complex variations, however, and most of us use tenses correctly by imitation, even though it's difficult to explain just how we do it.

Examples:

1. *Present tense:* The city is beautiful.

2. *Past tense:* The city was beautiful.

3. *Future tense:* The city will be beautiful.

An important form of the past tense often not used when it should be is the *past perfect,* which indicates an action or condition completed *before another past* action or condition—a sort of further past.

Examples:

1. The city   *had been*   beautiful before they
           (past perfect tense)

   bombed   it.
   (past tense)

2. Molly   *had loved*   him before he   *popped*
       (past perfect tense)   (past tense)

   his gum.

In writing, it is important not to change tenses needlessly as you proceed through a story or account of events. Change tense only when you have a reason for it.

Examples:

1. Wrong: The teacher *entered* the room and *starts* teaching while the class still *talked.*

2. Right: The teacher *entered* the room and *started* teaching while the class *was* still *talking.*

3. Right: The teacher *enters* the room and *starts* teaching while the class *is* still *talking.*

that, which, who-whose-whom

The *relative pronouns* "that," "which," "who," "whose," and "whom" relate the CLAUSE of which they are the first word to another word or other words in a sentence.

Examples:

1. Don't bite the hand *that* feeds you.

2. I dislodged a rock, *which* rattled down the slope.

3. The woman *who* shot him was insane.

4. Those astronauts *whom* I met didn't know how to swim.

5. The dog *whose* tooth was missing had left it in my right leg.

In general, use *who* and *whom* when referring to people, *which* when referring to things, and *that* when referring to either people or things. Use *whom* when it functions as the object of a VERB or PREPOSITION.

Example:

... *whom* I met ...; to *whom*
(obj. of vb.) (subj.) (verb)   (prep.) (obj. of prep.)

I was talking

See also WHO-WHOM.

thesaurus

A thesaurus is a REFERENCE BOOK of related words grouped by ideas. It contains lists of synonyms (words that have similar meanings) and, often, antonyms (words that have opposite meanings). A thesaurus is especially useful when you are looking for a word to express the precise meaning you have in mind but can't quite pinpoint. By far the best-known thesauruses are based on the work of Peter Mark Roget, pronounced *Rozhay* (1779-1869).

titles

Other things being equal, a composition is improved by a good title. It arouses the interest of readers; it gives the paper a label which makes it easier to identify and remember. It's worth more than a moment of your time to think up a title or label for each paper you write.

See CAPITALIZATION, 9, for its application to titles. When writing the titles of books or magazines, underline (italicize) them; when writing the titles of chapters or articles within books or magazines, enclose them in quotation marks.

Example:
Chapter 5 of H. G. Wells' *The War of the Worlds* is called "The Heat Ray."

topic sentences   see PARAGRAPHS.

transitions
A writer or speaker must lead the reader or listener from one idea or section to the next in a way that is easy and pleasant to follow. Paragraphs should succeed each other in some kind of comfortable progression. Often the succession of ideas and paragraphs is made easier to understand by the use of *transitional words or phrases*. For example, if you have written about one aspect of a subject and are ready to switch to a contrasting aspect, you can signal the switch with such phrases or words as "on the other hand" and "however." However, if you want the reader to understand that you are continuing along the same lines, a word such as "furthermore" or a phrase such as "in addition" helps to clue him in.

The following useful transitional words and phrases are roughly grouped by the function they serve. Notice that some of them serve more than one function.

> *adding:* also, another, at the same time, first (second, third), in addition, in the same way, moreover, next
>
> *concluding:* at last, finally, in conclusion, therefore
>
> *continuing:* also, another, at the same time, furthermore, indeed, in the first (second, third) place, in the same way, meantime, then [be careful not to overuse this one], too
>
> *contrasting:* but, however, on the other hand, one . . . another
>
> *exemplifying:* for example, that is
>
> *explaining or amplifying:* also, consequently, for example, furthermore, in addition, indeed, in fact, moreover, of course, that is, therefore, too

T

transitive verbs   see VERBS, A.

typing

Typing is a very useful skill if you are to do well in any subject that requires a lot of writing. Many people find it quite easy to learn to type while they are of school age and able to establish habits easily. I would recommend that you learn to touch-type as early as possible if you have a serious interest in academic work. Take a course if one is offered by your school, find one in the community (perhaps during the summer), or get a book of typing lessons and learn on your own.

When you type papers for school or for publication, leave double spaces between lines (it's much easier for teachers to read and correct and for you to revise), leave a left-hand margin of an inch and a half, and avoid crowding.

However, don't become so dependent on typing that you lose the skill of writing by hand quickly and legibly, since this, of course, is what you will have to do in exams, tests, and other writing in school.

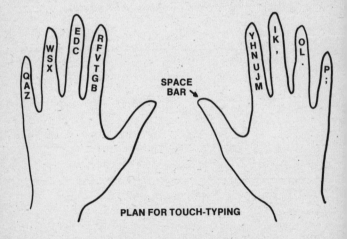

PLAN FOR TOUCH-TYPING

underlining

Underlining is used to show that a word is used in a special way. In printed materials ITALICS are used instead of underlining.

1. Underline the titles of books, magazines, your own compositions, the names of ships, works of art, and the like. (But use QUOTATION MARKS for titles of chapters, stories, or articles in books or magazines.)

Examples:

1. How to Achieve Competence in English is the title of this book.
2. He flew on Jetline's Phantom Whisper II to Paris to see the Mona Lisa.

2. Underline—but rarely—for emphasis.

3. Underline a word referred to as a word or a letter as a letter.

Examples:

1. He used love three times in the sentence and lover twice.
2. Don't leave the e out of courageous.

4. Underline foreign words and phrases.

Example:

If you study Latin, you'll understand the phrase e pluribus unum on your coins.

usage see GRAMMAR, C.

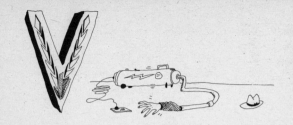

variety in sentences   see SENTENCE VARIETY.

verbal

A verbal is a word formed from a verb but used as another PART OF SPEECH. The three kinds of verbals are GERUNDS, INFINITIVES, and PARTICIPLES.

verbs

A verb is one of the PARTS OF SPEECH. As most commonly defined, a verb is a word that expresses action or state of being. Most verbs express action—such as *shout, jump, crush, pound, wriggle, snort,* and *push*—as well as "mental" actions—for example, *think, believe, understand, sympathize,* and *hate.*

Verbs, and no other class of words, change TENSE by adding endings, by grouping with auxiliaries or by changing form.

Examples:

1. I *speak*   I *spoke*   I have *spoken*
                                    (aux.)

2. He *listens.*   They *listened.*   We shall *listen.*
                                                       (aux.)

Verbs are usually the most important part of the PREDICATE in a SENTENCE.

A FRAME TEST for verbs is: "Let's _____ it."
                                             (verb)

Any word that sounds right or makes sense in the blank can be a verb; in terms of the frame sentence it must be singular in number and in the present tense.

V

A. *Transitive and intransitive verbs*

1. Transitive verbs are verbs that take an object (see DIRECT OBJECTS). That is, the action of the verb is received by a grammatical object.

Examples:

1. The rhino *charged* the *man.*
   (trans. vb.)   (object)

2. He *spoke* his *thoughts.*
   (trans. vb.)   (object)

2. Intransitive verbs are verbs whose action does not carry across to something else (a direct object) but is complete in itself.

Examples:

1. Alfred is *snoring.*
   (intr. vb.)

2. The talking dog *spoke* too long.
   (intr. vb.)

3. Night *fell* and I *trembled.*
   (intr. vb.)   (intr. vb.)

NOTE: Many verbs can be used both transitively and intransitively.

Examples:

1. Joe *feels* stubborn. [intransitive]

2. Joe *feels* the squishy mud. [transitive]

3. Cleopatra *loved* well. [intransitive]

4. Cleopatra *loved* Antony. [transitive]

B. *Linking verbs*

Linking verbs, in old-fashioned grammars called *copulative verbs* (because they couple), are a special subclass of verbs. They do not express action but link elements in SENTENCES that in some way refer to the same thing.

Examples: subject   linking verb   complement

1. Jim   is   a bum.   [Jim = bum]
                (noun)

2. George   became   a cripple.
                        (noun)

[George = cripple]

3. Jim   was   handsome.
   (adj.)

   [Jim = handsome; handsome Jim]

4. Garbage   smells   lovely to pigs.
   (adj.)

   [garbage = lovely; lovely garbage—to pigs!]

NOTES:

1. The word that appears in the predicate (see SENTENCES) and is linked to the subject by the linking verb is called the complement—the element that completes the sentence. In the first sentence above the complement is *bum*. Complements can be either NOUNS or ADJECTIVES.

2. There are only a very few common linking verbs in English. By far the most common is the verb *be*. You don't very often use it in that form except in such sentences as "Be brave"; "be a friend to me." But the verb *be* has several common forms: *am, is, are, was, were.* The other common linking verbs are: *appear, become, feel,* grow,* look, remain, seem, smell,* sound,* taste.** The verbs marked with an asterisk (*) can also be used as nonlinking verbs.

Examples:

   as linking verb   *as nonlinking verb*

1. The lamb *feels* sick. The baby *feels* the   lamb.
        (complement)   (obj. of verb)

2. Soup *tastes* delicious. Bob *tastes* the   soup.
        (complement)   (obj. of verb)

A FRAME TEST for linking verbs is: They _____
(linking verb)
nice.

C. *Auxiliary verbs*

Auxiliary verbs, sometimes called *helping verbs,* combine with main verbs to show change of TENSE or time.

Examples:

1. George   *is*   *swimming* in the bathtub. [pres-
        (auxil.) (main vb.)
   ent tense]

2. The alligator   *was*   *tossed* by the waves.
        (auxil.)   (main vb.)
   [past tense]

3. Mabel *will*   *claim*   the victory. [future
     (auxil.)   (main verb)

tense]

4. Mr. Jones *had*   *been*   *doing* the laundry.
      (auxil.) (auxil.)   (main vb.)

[past perfect tense]

About twenty auxiliaries are used in English in various combinations.

    am, is, are, was, were, be, been
    can, could
    do, does, did
    has, have, had
    may, might
    shall, will, should, would

Some of the auxiliaries can also be used as main verbs.

Examples:

1. Frank *did* write yesterday.
      (auxil.)

2. Frank   *did*   his homework.
    (main verb)

3. Poor swimmers *have* drowned out there.
      (auxil.)

4. Poor swimmers   *have*   trouble with the
       (main verb)

undertow.

See also PARTS OF SPEECH; PRINCIPAL PARTS; IRREGULAR VERBS; TENSES.

vocabulary building

A person with a large vocabulary tends to succeed better at communication than does a person with a small one, but that's not to say that making an intensive effort to build your vocabulary will make you more likely to succeed in life. It's curiosity, interest, intelligence, observation, richness of experience, reading, listening, and good memory that tend to produce both ample vocabularies and successful people.

V

The average person learns most of the 30,000–40,000 words whose meaning he or she recognizes by hearing or reading them in context or simply absorbing them without conscious effort (see LANGUAGE). The best way to a good vocabulary, therefore, is to read a great deal and to participate in a lot of good talk. There are relatively few words that we learn permanently by purposefully referring to DICTIONARIES or keeping word lists. However, even those extra few are of value, and no one will make a mistake by working on developing a larger vocabulary. Here are some suggestions of how to do it.

1. Read plenty of good books. When you come across a new word, or a new meaning of an old word, stop and see if you can understand it from its CONTEXT (the words around it). If you can't, and if you can manage it without interrupting the thought of the book too much, look it up in a dictionary or ask somebody and then repeat its meaning to yourself a couple of times. If you are really conscientious, write the word and its meaning in a personal vocabulary list—preferably using it in a sentence. (You can use the blank lined pages at the end of each letter section of this book for your list, or you can keep a special vocabulary notebook.) Go over the list from time to time. Further, try to use a new word in writing or conversation a few times over the next several days.

2. Listen to good talk and be alert to new words you hear or to new meanings of words you already know. Then treat them just as you do new words you read.

3. Learn and be alert to parts of words: PREFIXES, SUFFIXES, and ROOTS. Knowing them enables you to make intelligent guesses about the meanings of words.

4. If you are studying a foreign language, be alert for words in that language which relate to words in English. English has inherited or borrowed much of its vocabulary of 500,000–600,000 words from Latin, Greek, French, Spanish, and German. Generally the shorter,

V

easier ones come from Germanic tongues, while the longer, more elaborate ones are derived from the others.

voice

In grammar, voice denotes the form of the verb that shows the relation between the subject and verb. The *active voice* means that the subject does the action; the *passive voice* mains that the subject is acted upon by the verb.

Examples:

Active voice.	1. John *destroyed* the picture.
	2. Gloria *wanted* a medium-rare steak.
	3. Many people *think* the idea is no good.
Passive voice.	1. The picture *was destroyed* by John.
	2. A medium-rare steak *was wanted* by Gloria.
	3. It *is thought* by many people that the idea is no good.

The active voice is usually more forceful and direct than the passive, while the passive expresses greater caution and is sometimes awkward and ponderous (as in the second example). When in doubt, choose the active voice. Don't hide behind the passive. If you think something, write, "I think," not "It is thought that..." The passive voice conceals the "doer" of the deed.

_____

_____

_____

_____

_____

which; that   see THAT; WHICH.

who-whom

Who and *whom* are *relative* PRONOUNS or *interrogative pronouns*—pronouns that ask a question. (See THAT; WHICH.) The word *who* is the subjective CASE or form; *whom* is the objective case. When you use the pronoun as a grammatical subject, use *who*.

> *Examples:*
> 1. *Who* *went* out the door just then?
>   (subj.)   (verb)
>
> 2. The person *who* I think *did* it escaped
>   (subj.)   (verb)
>   over the wall.

When you use the pronoun as a grammatical object either of a PREPOSITION or of a VERB, use *whom*.

> *Examples:*
> 1. *With* *whom* did Molly share her rocking
>   (prep.)   (obj. of prep.)
>   chair?
>
> 2. The person *whom* she *strangled* was
>   (object of vb.)   (verb)
>   never seen again.

In informal speech—most of the speaking we all do—the word *whom* is gradually disappearing, although there are still many people who like to hear it used correctly, particularly after a preposition. In writing, however, *whom* is alive and well, and you should know when and how to use it.

word order   see GRAMMAR, B.

W

word skills   see STUDY SKILLS.

writing for whom?

Let's face it, most writing in most schools is done for teachers. That's too bad, because most of the writing in life outside of school is done for different audiences. However, a good teacher can teach you how to write better; if you are in school, therefore, keep writing and try to benefit from the instruction you are given. If you find the instruction limiting rather than helpful, learn what you can from it and do other writing for yourself, or submit it to other people if you'd like other reactions.

You will do best in school if you are clear for whom you are writing. Discuss this question in class before starting on an assignment. Some of the "audiences" or readerships for whom you might write are

1. *yourself*—as in a confidential diary;
2. *a trusted adult*—as in a letter or even an assignment;
3. *a trusted friend of your own age*—as in a letter;
4. *yourself*, but with the knowledge that what you write will be *read by your teacher*—as in a journal that is handed in periodically;
5. *a teacher as partner*—as in a paper that you're glad to share, to which you may expect some reaction and comment but which will not be marked;
6. *a teacher as "master,"* when you understand that the teacher probably knows more than you do about writing and will "correct" the paper, probably MARK it and suggest REVISIONS to help you write better;
7. *a teacher as examiner*—as in a test or exam, when you're writing to show how well you can do and to get as good a mark as you can;

8. *your classmates*—as when you know that your paper may be read aloud by you or your teacher and may be discussed by the class or a group in the class, and your main task is to interest them;

9. *a public audience*—as when you write an article for the school paper or magazine or when you are assigned to write as if for the general public, whom you do not know personally.

Probably most writing in English classes is done for the teacher as "master" and for your classmates, often for both at the same time.

_____

_____

_____

_____

_____

_____

_____

_____

_____

_____

_____

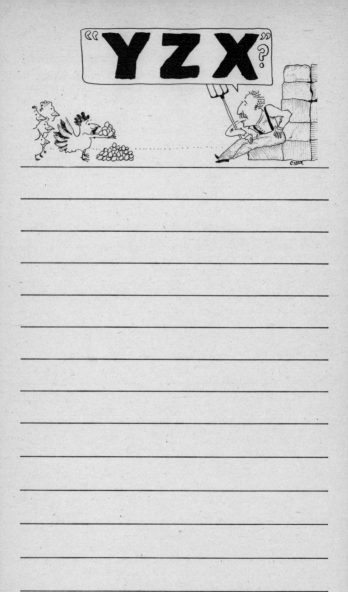